Wheat, Weeds, and the Reform of Christianity

How The Teachings of Men Have Distorted The Teachings of Jesus

Adam Leonard

Egress Publishing
Sarasota, FL

Egress Publishing

ISBN 13: 978-0692803936
ISBN 10: 0692803939
Printed in the U.S.A.
Printed January 2017

To Shirley belovéd,
my Muse, my Wife, my Love, my Life

Table of Contents

Introduction:

Part 1:
"Weeds" in the Old Testament / Hebrew Bible

Part 2:
"Weeds" in the New Testament

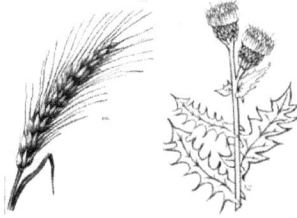

Introduction:
Separating Wheat From Weeds
– A New Method –

"The teachings of Jesus have been distorted by the teachings of men."

This thesis is hardly new, but the method this book uses to separate "wheat" from "weeds" … to distinguish between the teachings of Jesus and the teachings of Men which distort them … is dramatically new.

Over the last half century much has been learned about how our brain functions, and for the first time in human history there is hard evidence to explain why we consistently behave the irrational ways we do.

We can now examine Scripture with the benefit of this insight into human nature, and discern more clearly where the hand of Man – or as Jeremiah put it, "the lying pen of the Scribes" – is at work undermining the Word of God.

These "teachings of Men" are discernible both within Scripture and within our institutionalized interpretations of Scripture … our doctrines. They subtly diminish God's goodness and power to act, and imply God has given favored groups – those who interpret Scripture rightly – power over others. Such teachings, in both Scripture and doctrine, are the "weeds" planted by Men which need to be recognized and downplayed in favor of the "wheat" planted by God. Scripture cannot and should not be altered, but our understanding of it needs to grow so that we can recognize where Man's innate tendencies have allowed self-serving weeds to take root.

Jesus taught that he wanted his followers "to be one, that the world might believe." But instead of oneness Christianity presents to the world a medieval patchwork of denominational and non-denominational fiefdoms, all quarreling and fighting over nuances of scriptural interpretation. Whenever we have tried to merge the doctrines and practices of two or more denominations the efforts have almost always failed, and in the few times they succeeded dissenting members broke off to create even more denominations. ... It's no wonder we've essentially given up on trying to make Christianity "one."

Now, however, the growing understanding of how our brain functions is enabling us to end the impasse by recognizing that Man's quarreling, self-destructive behavior is the result of unconscious "programming" that predisposes us to behave as warring, tribal territorial animals ... just as described in the Hebrew Bible/Old Testament.

This book incorporates the new knowledge to show why the teachings of Jesus really *are* the means of salvation for Mankind, why we routinely distort them to our own tribe's advantage, and how Christianity can overcome this innate tribalism to finally become "one."

Because public awareness of scientific discoveries often lags the events by decades or more, I wrote the book "*Man by Nature: The Hidden Programming Controlling Human Behavior*" to publicize the significance of recent brain discoveries and to lay a foundation for this book. I had come to realize our religious behavior could not be understood unless we first understood the tribal territorial animal nature underlying it.

"*Man by Nature*" described how brain research with split-brain patients led to the discovery of a unique left-brain function that enables us to be tribal territorial animals largely controlled by instincts, but to nonetheless believe we are rationally choosing to do the irrational things we do.

The research showed – repeatedly – that whenever we do anything not consciously planned, as when motivated by instincts, this function automatically generates a conscious explanation for our actions and a conviction that the explanation is true. The scientists discovering this function called it the "interpreter," since it provides an interpretive explanation of our behavior, but in "*Man by Nature*" I began referring to it with the more descriptive and entertaining term, the "Great Explainer."

It is not possible to overstate the importance of the discovery of the Great Explainer. Although it is acknowledged our DNA is about ninety-eight percent the same as chimpanzees, and we periodically admit various aspects of our behavior are "animal-like," we have never taken our animal nature seriously enough to identify it as the primary cause of Mankind's constant warring. The reason we have not is that we cannot detect when animal instincts are affecting our behavior: the Great Explainer generates "rational" reasons for the behavior and we believe them implicitly, so it appears there is no instinctive behavior involved – we are totally blind to it.

Now, because of the incontestable proof that the Great Explainer exists and deceives us, we can – and must – accept this reality: we are tribal territorial animals programmed to war and quarrel with one another, and this programming is the source of Mankind's consistent irrational behavior … including our feuding religious factions.

… This emphatically does *not* mean, however, that our behavior is *predestined*, only that it is *predisposed* by our tribal instincts. We, unique among animals, have the capacity to override our instincts and have done so throughout our existence. The claim that acknowledging our instincts would justify brutish behavior is unfounded, and should not be used as an excuse to justify denying human instincts.

Once we accept the reality of our underlying tribal territorial animal nature, we can then observe a significant, uniquely human tribal trait: *human tribes have evolved to be based on shared tribal beliefs, and to treat tribal beliefs as "territory" to be defended as fiercely and irrationally as actual territory.* This singular observation explains why humans have proven incapable, historically and presently, of resolving differences of belief rationally, whether the beliefs are religious or secular (e.g. ideological.)

Like it or not, the scales have been removed from our eyes and everything we thought we knew about human nature has to be reexamined with our new insight – including religion. It is my conviction that this reexamination will strengthen Judeo-Christianity by deemphasizing doctrines that are based on "teachings of men," doctrines that have weakened Christianity's witness to the world and provided excuses to dismiss it.

"*Man by Nature*" demonstrated that it is not *religious* beliefs but beliefs *per se* that are the cause of the world's troubles: atheist regimes have killed as many millions in the name of secular beliefs as religions have for religious beliefs. ... It also held out hope that Man's ineradicable spiritual instinct might eventually enable us to overcome our predisposition to war. The concluding paragraph in the chapter *Spiritual Man* stated:

> *This spiritual, altruistic idea that Man's individual and collective purpose is to achieve Goodness – to become as loving and caring across tribal boundaries as within tribal boundaries – provides the only hope that Man will not eventually destroy itself. ... But until religions, all religions, reform themselves and begin caring more for Goodness than for dogma, doctrines, and rituals ... there really is no hope.*

This is not encouraging, for the odds are great against even one of the world's major religions reforming itself, let alone all. Compulsive tribal behavior – blind allegiance to tribal beliefs –

inevitably trumps reason, and whenever religious reforms are attempted the reformers are branded as heretics or apostates and banished from the tribe ... to start yet another tribe and branch of religion. This pattern is particularly painful and embarrassing for Christianity, since it directly defies Jesus' injunction "to be one, that the world might believe."

⊷⧼⧽⊶

What are we to say then, that because it appears hopeless to overcome our wired-in animal nature, we should not even try? As Paul would say, "God forbid!" It is our purpose and glory in life to strive for perfection ... to "become perfect, even as your Father in Heaven is perfect." The teachings of Jesus, as you will see, really *are* the answers to the world's problems, for they address the core problems of human nature – of human tribalism – that have plagued Mankind since Creation. As we become more and more aware of how our tribal territorial animal programming drives our persistent, consistent human failings, we will also become more and more aware of how Jesus' teachings enable overcoming them.

The human struggle is, and always has been, between our species' animal nature and our transcendent spiritual nature – between "*the Flesh*" and "*the Spirit*"; this is discernible throughout Scripture. Jesus taught that God allows the wheat and the weeds to grow together and, as will be discussed, did not exempt Scripture from this truth: God-inspired and Man-inspired ideas mingle and clash in every book of the Bible. The most important and interesting battles in the Hebrew Bible/Old Testament are not the physical battles between ethnic tribes, but the ever-present internal ones between the schools of prophets, competing priesthoods, and the kings and courts of Judah and Israel, all vying for influence and dominance. These struggles may be less obvious than the physical battles, but they are infinitely more significant: they reveal the intrinsic conflict between God and Man. Passages that seemingly praise God often misrepresent Him to Man's advantage.

When we study the Christian New Testament things do not change: God is still God, Man is still Man, and the teachings of men still intermingle with and attempt to negate the Word of God and the teachings of Jesus.

Can the two be separated? ... I say, "Yes," and the purpose of this book is to begin the process of separating them. Neither the nature of God nor the nature of Man changes, and this unchangeability allows us to detect when Man's characteristic tribal behavior is influencing Scripture by scattering weeds among the wheat.

⋘◦⋙

This book is composed of two parts:

Part 1 demonstrates our tribal nature at work scattering weeds throughout the Hebrew Bible – the Christian Old Testament. The phrase, "our tribal nature," does not mean only that we instinctively and naturally form tribes, but that all human tribes have the same tribal traits that cause us to consistently behave in the same flawed, self-destructive ways; these flaws are evident throughout Scripture.

The first chapter of Part 1 reviews the characteristic human tribal traits derived in *"Man by Nature: The Hidden Programming Controlling Human Behavior,"* and the following chapters demonstrate those traits affecting human behavior throughout the Hebrew Bible.

Part 2 demonstrates our tribal nature continuing at work scattering weeds throughout the Christian New Testament. It shows how the teachings of Jesus directly address the human flaws arising from our tribal traits, but how our tribal traits have nonetheless succeeded in intermingling "teachings of Men" with the teachings of Jesus. It presents evidence that two fundamental doctrines of Christianity have the handprints of Man all over them, and could not possibly have been taught by Jesus.

The final chapter in Part 2, *What Christianity Should Teach*, describes the steps necessary for Christianity – all of Christianity – to reform itself and demonstrate to the world that the teachings of Jesus *do* provide the means of saving Mankind … from itself.

Let the journey begin.

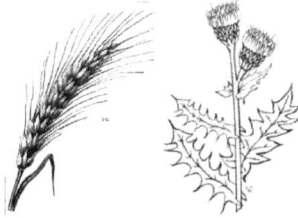

&⊷ Part 1 &⊷

"Weeds" in the
Hebrew Bible / Old Testament

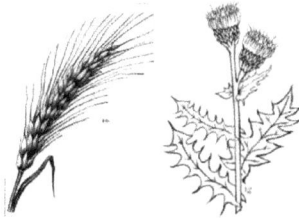

Chapter 1.
Human Tribal Traits

Humans, like all other animal species, are programmed by instincts to behave in characteristic ways. It is useful to describe this programming in terms analogous to computer programming as being "hardwired," "firmwired," or "softwired" depending upon how difficult it is to alter the programming once it has been "written." Hardwired programming cannot be altered, ever; firmwired programming can be altered but only with difficulty; and softwired programming (programs the computer simply "runs") can be altered relatively easily.

In humans, the species programming causing us to be *homo sapiens* is hardwired and has remained essentially unchanged throughout our existence; the programming we develop to walk, talk, and cope within our environment is firmwired and can be changed only with intense effort, often requiring physical or psychological therapy; the programming we develop consciously through learning … our *ideas*: our literature, art, and architecture; our music, math, and medicine; our sciences, philosophies, and psychologies … is softwired and easily and regularly changed.

There is one extremely important exception to this last generality, however, and that is when an *idea* become elevated to a *belief*. While ideas are softwired and can be discussed rationally, beliefs become firmwired and cannot: we defend our beliefs with the same fierce irrationality that we do our territory. The emotions of rage and outrage that we experience when our *beliefs* are violated are exactly the same emotions we experience when our *territory* is violated. For example, the outrage that wells up when watching the despised leader of an opposition party giving a speech violating our beliefs is the same outrage that wells up as "road rage" when another driver violates our right-of-way, our territory.

Our instincts pit us against those having differing beliefs and makes it difficult, almost impossible, for us to resolve our differences and live in peace. While we cannot prevent our emotions from occurring, we can – and must – learn to recognize them as stemming from the unconscious instincts goading our behavior, and consequentially develop a sheath of cultural beliefs to constrain them.

While our unconscious instincts are inaccessible to us, our consequential human behavior is observable and can be described with a set of "human tribal traits." Our basic tribal traits are shared with other tribal territorial animals, particularly primates, but due to our uniqueness in having language, conscious thought, and beliefs, we also have unique homo sapiens tribal traits dependent upon our enhanced abilities.

The basic tribal traits, possessed in common with other tribal territorial animals are:

- an instinct to form tribes;
- an instinct to form hierarchical, usually male-dominant social structures within our tribes;
- an instinct to be supportive, protective, and even self-sacrificing for those within our tribe;
- an instinct to treat other tribes of our species as rivals and to fight with them for dominance.

An instinct to form tribes

Paraphrasing John Donne, "No man is tribeless, no man survives alone." We compulsively form not only national tribes, but political tribes, religious tribes, social tribes, workplace tribes, sports fan tribes, family tribes, etc., etc., etc.

An instinct to form hierarchical social structures

Like most primates and most other tribal animals we instinctively form hierarchical, usually male-dominant social structures … pyramidal power structures controlled by "Alpha" leaders.

An instinct to be supportive, protective, and even self-sacrificing

Ethologists observing and documenting the social behavior of other primates have established that they, too, demonstrate our most praised and prized social traits: comforting, caring, sharing, tenderness … nurturing the young, old, and injured, coming to each other's aid and defense … even altruism. All of this is accomplished through programmed instincts and without the need of language, conscious thought, or the ability to form beliefs.

It is probable that humans and other animals experience instincts in the same way – as "feelings" that motivate actions – but in humans our Great Explainer thoroughly masks our instincts by generating implicitly believed conscious explanations for our feelings and subsequent behavior … allowing us to believe we are free of instincts.

An instinct to treat other tribes of our species as rivals

Just as it is natural for chimpanzee troops, wolf packs, and brown rat clans to fight among themselves, it is unfortunately natural for human tribes to do so too. The entire history of Man is a history of warring tribes and empires: the Egyptians, Assyrians, Babylonians, Greeks, Romans, Germanics, Islamics, Mongolians, Chinese dynasties, Aztecs, Mayans, European colonial empires, the United States, Nazi Germany, Imperial Japan, and the late and unlamented Soviet Union. (And as of this writing, fundamentalist Islamic tribes are gathering power and threatening yet another world conflict, while Russia and China are resuming the expansion of their border claims.)

Whenever an empires falls, its constituent tribes resume fighting for dominance: this has been demonstrated consistently from the breakdown of the Greek and Roman empires to the breakdown of Colonialism and the Soviet Union.

☙❧

While these basic tribal territorial animal traits – forming tribes, having hierarchical social structures, being caring and supportive of tribemembers, and perceiving other tribes as enemies – are shared with other tribal territorial animals, our uniqueness in having language, conscious thought, and beliefs, allows us to have unique homo sapiens tribal traits dependent upon these enhanced abilities:

- Human tribes are based on common tribal beliefs;
- We treat our tribal beliefs as "territory" to be fiercely defended;
- We try to impose our tribal beliefs on other tribes, by war if necessary;
- We are unconsciously biased by our beliefs;
- We are inherently blind to our bias toward our beliefs;
- We stereotype opposing tribes, then caricature all their members as being like their extremists;
- We make "scapegoat" enemies of the tribes who oppose us, and routinely slander them; we may see them as non-human to justify exterminating them;
- Whenever our beliefs are opposed, we migrate them to extreme positions;
- We compulsively make up explanations for things unknown;
- We compulsively create law codes to govern behavior;
- We use our law codes to impose our tribal beliefs;
- We use stories to pass on tribal beliefs and culture;
- We choose only one of competing explanations to believe, and then deny the others.

Human tribes are based on common tribal beliefs

While it's conventionally assumed human tribes are based upon clans or race (since most early tribes started that way), observation reveals that human tribes are actually, ultimately, based upon common beliefs: we recognize as tribe members only those who accept and adhere to our beliefs; members who question tribal beliefs, whether as a heretic or a prophet, are rejected by the tribe – a wolf in sheep's clothing! – and non-members who adopt our beliefs may be welcomed in. A tribe's beliefs typically include a self-defining "noble cause" that justifies the tribe's existence, and a scapegoat enemy tribe that's blamed for opposing the noble cause.

We treat our tribal beliefs as "territory" to be fiercely defended

When Man evolved language and the ability to store memories and form beliefs, our already existing territorial defense programming was extended to include beliefs, to treat our beliefs as territory. This hypothesis can't be proven, but the evidence that we defend our beliefs as fiercely and irrationally as territory is overwhelming: we can discuss ideas rationally, but not our beliefs, neither religious nor secular.

We try to impose our tribal beliefs on other tribes

Since tribes are based on common beliefs, the way to dominate other tribes is to impose our tribe's beliefs on them. Thus Liberals vie against Conservatives, Catholics against Protestants, Republicans against Democrats, Denominations against Non-denominations, hedonists against ascetics, etc., etc..

National tribes also vie to impose their beliefs on one another, but first need a territorial base: after securing their territory they can begin "empire building" by conquering other tribes' territories and imposing their beliefs.

While political, religious, and other subtribes don't engage in physical warfare as routinely as national tribes, they nonetheless are susceptible to doing so if their ideologies become strong enough. If a subtribe's ideology (beliefs) become more important to them than their national tribal beliefs, they ignore the dangers of destroying the national tribe and attempt to have their subtribe's beliefs become dominate. ... As of this writing the Republican and Democrat political parties in America each accuse the other of this fault.

We are unconsciously biased by our beliefs

We unconsciously reject information opposing our beliefs, and embrace information supporting them. This "confirmation bias," has been observed and commented upon for hundreds of years, but only recently has become explainable.

Brain research using fMRI (functional Magnetic Resonance Imaging) has shown that our brain processes ideas subconsciously by presenting them in parallel to arrays of modules for evaluation, merging the results to generate an emotional cue indicating whether the idea supports or challenges our existing beliefs, and activating the Great Explainer to generate a string of conscious "rational" arguments justifying the emotion.

The subconscious evaluation unerringly detects how well an idea agrees with our existing beliefs, and the emotional cue that is generated – approval, acceptance, annoyance, anger, rage, outrage – reflects that evaluation. Thus we are innately biased in favor of ideas or data that support our beliefs and against ideas or data that challenge them.

We are inherently blind to our bias toward our beliefs

Because the evaluation of new ideas against existing beliefs takes place subconsciously all we experience is the resulting emotion, and because the Great Explainer automatically supplies implicitly believed conscious arguments to rationalize such emotions, we consciously believe we have judged the idea rationally and experienced the emotion as a result of our reasoning – exactly the opposite of what actually occurs.

We stereotype opposing tribes, then caricature all their members as being like their extremists

A stereotype is "an oversimplified, widely accepted, and typically biased image or description of a group or class of people." We do this automatically, unconsciously, since it's part of our wired-in means of classifying, simplifying, and comprehending the world's myriad entities.

A caricature is "a gross distortion of the character and/or characteristics of another person or group, usually for the purpose of mocking them, and often quite vicious." Politics and religion bring out the tribal worst in us and provide the motivations for our more despicable stereotyping and caricaturing of others.

When another tribe becomes an opponent, we pick out the worst behavior exhibited by the worst of them – their extremists – and caricature the whole tribe as being like that. Thus political parties, religious denominations, and sports fans routinely "trash" their opponents as personified evil.

We make "scapegoat" enemies of the tribes who oppose us, and routinely slander them

Whatever tribe opposes our beliefs, particularly our noble cause, becomes a "scapegoat enemy" and is thereafter blamed for all setbacks to tribal interests; they become the embodiment of Evil, and are regularly maligned and slandered with the utter conviction the slurs are true. It seems that tribes *need* a scapegoat enemy, and if there is none, may create one. While we see and appreciate the wide variety of personalities and characters within our own tribe, we stereotype other tribes by describing them as all having the same characteristic appearance and traits.

Whenever our beliefs are opposed, we migrate them to extreme positions

When an opposing tribe questions or challenges a belief, we automatically make the belief more extreme, more absolute, and defend it more fiercely and blindly; we become polarized. This is evident, for example, in the positions we take on abortion and on biblical inerrancy.

We compulsively make up explanations for things unknown

An astonishing amount of what we think is "known" is simply made up. If we don't know the explanation for something, we make one up – out of nothing – and if it sounds at all plausible, we immediately forget we made it up and believe it to be Truth. It is only now, with the discovery of our brain's Great Explainer function, that we can understand this phenomenon.

Our compulsion to make up explanations for things unknown is evident in both superstition and science. Whenever one event follows another, or occurs under some circumstance, we routinely explain the latter as happening *because* of the preceding event or circumstance. When we add the step of testing our conclusions to see if they are repeatable, however, suddenly we're no longer superstitious but are now "Scientists" using the Scientific Method.

We compulsively create law codes to govern behavior

Human societies have always made laws. This is demonstrably true at least since Man learned to write, for the oldest surviving writings from ancient civilizations contain both snippets and whole bodies of law; the Code of Hammurabi and Torah of Moses are the best-known examples of the latter. All of these laws, recorded over the millennia, reveal that Man's nature has not changed: we have continuously demonstrated the same propensity for killing, stealing, deceiving, cheating, slandering, and fornicating. Every law we make not only admits that someone has done what that law prohibits, but that we expect Man is likely to do it again unless prevented. ... Laws, like bars on a zoo cage, attempt to restrain the animal within: if the animal isn't dangerous, why are the bars needed? Clearly our laws indict us as being flawed creatures, inherently predisposed to self-destructive behavior.

Not only do our laws reveal much about our nature, so do the ways we implement and enforce them:

- We institutionalize laws into a game played by lawyers and judges, forgetting that Justice (Justice!) was once the goal;
- We enforce laws selectively: stringently upon our foes, leniently upon our friends;
- We treat favored laws as immutable absolutes;
- We forget the original intent of our laws, and subsequently misapply them.

We use our law codes to impose our tribal beliefs

Laws are made and enforced (or not) by the national tribe or the dominant subtribe within it. They consequently impose the national or dominant subtribe's beliefs in the form of laws.

We use stories to pass on tribal beliefs and culture

It is recognized that for millennia storytelling was Man's primary means of passing on tribal history. No matter what your race, your ancestors sat around campfires or lodge fires and told and retold stories of their tribe's history: the stories described how the tribe came into being and told of its deities, heroes, villains, triumphs, and tragedies.

What hasn't been recognized, or at least hasn't been much commented upon, is that these stories have also been Man's primary means of passing on *behavioral standards* to succeeding generations ... of seeding the ideas desired and destined to become firmwired beliefs. The stories provide inspirational examples of bravery, character, morals, and ethics being courageously practiced by the tribe and tribe members in spite of opposition, and the backgrounds of the stories illustrate what a normative society should or shouldn't be. Thus, the stories reflect not only what the tribe was and is, but also what it will become.

We choose only one of competing explanations to believe, and then deny the others

As part of our innate drive to understand and explain our world, we naturally categorize, abstract, and simplify: we are predisposed to narrow down competing explanations, choose one, and enlist our confirmation bias to reject the others. In the extreme, if our chosen explanation is challenged by others we harden it into an absolute dictum that we defend blindly, even to the death.

⟳

This completes our summary of the predominant human tribal traits. The most important thing to note is that while we have the same underlying instincts as other primates, we uniquely have the ability to override our instincts with a sheath of cultural tribal beliefs. Although our behavior is *predisposed* by our instincts, it is not *predestined*. Not only do we have the *ability* to override our instincts, it can be argued that human tribes are *required* to evolve and maintain a set of cultural beliefs to restrain their instincts; all human societies, past and present, have done so.

In the next four chapters of Part 1, we will see our human tribal traits influencing behavior throughout all the books of the Hebrew Bible and allowing the scattering of weeds. In the final chapter of Part 1 we will see how the Wisdom books demonstrate cultural beliefs arising to govern our base instincts.

Chapter 2.
From the Beginning

When our ancient ancestors encountered the world for the first time, they were faced with the whole universe to explain. There was no precedent, no antecedents, and all they had to work with was what they were created with: five senses, instinctive feelings, instinctive behavior … and the Great Explainer.

Their efforts to explain how they and the universe came into being, why they felt and acted the way they did, and why other beings acted the way they did are recorded in the oldest teachings from all the world's religions. The teachings are cloaked in differing cultural guises, but all can be seen as resulting from the Great Explainer "explaining" their instinctive tribal feelings and behavior in the world they encountered.

Consistently there is a Creator God or gods who: created the Universe; created them (a favored tribe); created or allowed to diverge other (less favored) tribes; and who mandated a code of behavior that must be followed or suffer punishment. Since less favored tribes don't recognize or don't follow the Creator God (or gods) properly, it is incumbent on the favored tribe to correct them or kill them, to dominate or destroy. … No matter where on Earth our early forebears arose, their teachings codified and justified our instinctive tribal behavior: the teachings reflected both our good side – to be caring and self-sacrificing for tribemates – and our bad – to dominate or destroy rival tribes; history records that we have been in thralldom to this dual tribal nature ever since. We are both Good and Evil.

Why, it might be asked, did all tribes, everywhere, come up with a Creator God or gods to explain the existence of the universe? Have we an "instinct" to believe in a God or gods? Or, since it has been demonstrated that we are born with a functioning "knowledge" of basic physics (babies, for example, act surprised if an inanimate object seems to start moving all by itself), did it arise from the Great Explainer hypothesizing a *Cause* for Creation? ... We do not know, and our Great Explainer has been making up explanations ever since.

From the beginning in Genesis, the oldest portions of the Hebrew Bible unabashedly acknowledge our tribal nature and portray it accurately. Looking uncritically at the Bible stories, taking them as happening exactly as written, we see the descendants of Adam and Eve spread throughout the Middle East, settle, and give rise to all the known tribes, or "nations." The tribes are portrayed as constantly warring with one another simply as a matter of course, often with no "reasons" given or needed. Skim, for example, Genesis 14:1-9:

[1]And it came to pass in the days of Amraphel king of Shinar, Arioch king of Ellasar, Chedorlaomer king of Elam, and Tidal king of nations, [2]*that* they made war with Bera king of Sodom, Birsha king of Gomorrah, Shinab king of Admah, Shemeber king of Zeboiim, and the king of Bela (that is, Zoar). [3]All these joined together in the Valley of Siddim (that is, the Salt Sea). [4]Twelve years they served Chedorlaomer, and in the thirteenth year they rebelled. [5]In the fourteenth year Chedorlaomer and the kings that *were* with him came and attacked the Rephaim in Ashteroth Karnaim, the Zuzim in Ham, the Emim in Shaveh Kiriathaim, [6]and the Horites in their mountain of Seir, as far as El Paran, which *is* by the wilderness. [7]Then they turned back and came to En Mishpat (that *is*, Kadesh), and attacked all the country of the Amalekites, and also the Amorites who dwelt in Hazezon Tamar. [8]And the king of Sodom, the king of Gomorrah, the king of Admah, the king of Zeboiim, and the king of Bela (that *is*, Zoar) went out and joined together in battle in the Valley of Siddim [9]against Chedorlaomer king of Elam, Tidal king of [f]nations, Amraphel king of Shinar, and Arioch king of Ellasar—four kings against five.

Perhaps the most chilling verse in all the Bible is 2 Samuel 11 (repeated in 1 Chronicles 20) which so casually acknowledges our tribal compulsion to war and kill one another:

It happened in the spring of the year, at the time kings go out to battle ...

Thus the authors and editors of the Hebrew Bible, like the authors and editors of most other ancient religious texts, simply accepted that human tribes naturally, routinely war with one another for dominance. They documented our tribal evolution from patriarchal clans, to judge/warrior-led tribes, to king/priest-led "nations." All exhibited our tribal traits of hierarchical male-dominance, envisioned noble goals (serving Yahweh and imposing Yahwehism on others tribes), stereotyping, caricaturing and scapegoating rival tribes, and treating them as "non-people," as goyim. Tribal beliefs and customs were passed on as stories, first orally, then written, and law codes were developed to codify proper tribal behavior.

The only periods when Israel and its neighboring tribes were *not* portrayed as warring with one another were when larger tribes (initially Egypt, Assyria, and Babylon; eventually Greece and Rome) overpowered all of them, extracted tribute, and *imposed* peace. The larger tribes, too, are shown as constantly warring with one another for dominance, and "world peace" existed only when one succeeded in temporarily subjugating all the others and becoming an empire.

The Hebrew Bible also documents that as human tribes became larger they also became more complex, evolving subtribes that vied with one another for dominance within their national tribes. Rival warrior, royal, and religious factions emerged, and when not fighting for physical dominance they fought to embed their particular justifications and beliefs in the contemporary stories destined to become their peoples' history and legacy: it is this competition between internal subgroups (subtribes) that shaped the writing and editing of the Hebrew Bible in all its varied richness. This hidden, internal competition has been exposed, largely by Biblical scholars writing on the Documentary Hypothesis – the hypothesis that the five books of Moses developed over an extended period of time through the efforts of multiple editors redacting multiple source texts, culminating in the single work we have today.

The preeminent Hebrew Bible scholar and author, Richard Elliott Friedman, has written two books in particular that allow observing the competing factions within the royal courts, priesthoods, and guilds of prophets that were vying to have their version of history become the accepted version. The two books are *"Who Wrote the Bible?"*(1987) and *"The Bible with Sources Revealed"*(2005)." I will incorporate material from these two books extensively in the next three chapters, *"Priests vs. Priests,"* *"Kings and Courts,"* and *"Prophets and Spokesmen,"* as we examine human tribal traits at work in those settings. We will find that although science is just now gaining an understanding of the tribal instincts influencing our behavior, the Hebrew Bible had already recorded and documented them thoroughly. The struggles and infighting between competing tribes is discernible not only in the text itself, but also in the editing and canonizing.

The struggles still go on, only now they are not to determine what is *in* Scripture, but how Scripture should be *interpreted.* Thus the largest schism in Judaeo-Christianity today is not between major tribes (as it was between Jews, Catholics and Protestants in the past), but between those subtribes across all denominations who believe the Bible should be viewed as "the inerrant Word of God," and those who believe it should be viewed as "God inspired, but nonetheless containing teachings of Men."

Since we're now aware that when our beliefs are challenged we migrate them to more extreme, "stronger" positions, it is possible to understand how the "inerrant" position came about: when (some) nineteenth century theologians began using the nascent field of critical bible study to attack and weaken traditional beliefs – especially that Moses wrote the Torah – the response was to claim that not only did Moses write the Torah, he wrote it *inerrantly*, exactly as God had given it to him. This zealous rebuttal enabled Judeo-Christianity to endure and outlast the misguided attacks, and in the early twentieth century grew to become the "Fundamentalist" movement that continues to defend Christian orthodoxy to this day: they must be commended for that.

Defensive walls that are useful when being attacked by an enemy, however, become a liability when the community is no longer under attack: they then enclose the community and prevent its growth.

While Judeo-Christianity is certainly still under attack (and always will be, human nature being what it is) it is nonetheless likely that the early, unwarranted extrapolations of critical bible study that anti-religious factions used to try to destroy religion will never again have the power they did at that time. Critical bible study has instead proven to be an essential tool that enables understanding not only the many "contradictions" and "paradoxes" of the Bible but, more importantly, the complex, continuous, ever-enduring struggle between the Spirit of God and the Flesh of Man. It vastly strengthens the case that religion is not only vitally important to the wellbeing of Mankind, it may indeed be the *only* means of saving Mankind … from itself.

Can the defensive wall of inerrancy be safely dismantled, now that the existential threat from anti-religious groups has lessened, and now that inerrancy has become the major tribal division within Judeo-Christianity … a division defended with the fierce irrationality we reserve for our tribal territory and our tribal beliefs?

Your immediate, emotional reaction to this question is of course determined unconsciously by the beliefs you hold, and it will take an act of will for you to consciously, seriously question whether your instinctive reaction is what's best for Judeo-Christianity and the world, or whether it's simply what's best for those holding your beliefs …. for your tribe. Jesus prayed that his followers "may be one, that the world may believe," but Christians (too!) have historically ignored the word of God for the sake of their traditions.

My recommendation is that we all become "fundamentalists" in that we fiercely defend Judeo-Christianity against the attacks of militant secularism, but that we cease defending the superficial "teachings of Men" doctrines that divide us and instead defend the true fundamentals … the underlying "Spirit of God" truths that can unite us. While we argue over whether God dictated His underlying truths to Moses as one event or whether He inspired generations of believers to document the underlying truths, the world rightfully ridicules our blind disagreements and remains in denial that there *really are* underlying truths essential to the wellbeing and survival of Mankind.

✦

We'll begin now to examine how the teachings of Men intermingle and clash with the teachings of God throughout the Hebrew Bible, first with "*Priests vs. Priests*," followed by "*Kings and Courts*," and "*Prophets and Spokesmen*."

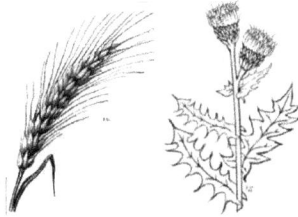

Chapter 3.
Priests vs. Priests

Scholarly writings on the Documentary Hypothesis describe the competing groups of Kings, Priests, and Prophets that struggled for dominance in the ancient Middle East. The Kings, with their generals, armies, and courts, vied for *territorial* dominance and power; the Priests and Prophets, with their attendants, guilds, and followers, vied for *theological* dominance and power. While all ostensibly followed and served God, their tribal allegiances' all too often caused them to pursue their tribal interests instead, and to malign and misrepresent God in the process.

Their struggles were inexorably intertwined: Kings had to be anointed by Priests to have legitimacy, and needed favorable prophesies (reviews, if you will) from the Prophets to maintain popular support; Kings, once king, however, could choose which of the vying Priesthoods to support and empower, and could banish or kill any Prophets who seriously opposed them; Prophets, in turn, could support the reigning King and/or Priesthood, or attack them, sometimes bringing their reigns to an end. Functionally the Prophets were the "watchdog press" of their day and, as in modern times, were susceptible to themselves becoming corrupted; thus there were additional ongoing struggles among the prophets and guilds of prophets over who was faithful and who corrupt.

The Documentary Hypothesis was initially concerned only with detecting and identifying the "primary source documents" that had become interwoven to produce the Five Books of Moses, but the search led to the realization that the strands didn't end with the five books but continued on, interwoven, throughout the historical books of the Hebrew Bible. Thus, the Bible's descriptions of the interactions between the Kings, Courts, Priests, and Prophets throughout the historical books provide continuing evidence of the opposing tribal tenets and biases of the authors of the source documents.

Four primary source documents were identified: they became known as the Jahwe ("Yahweh" in German), Elohim, Priestly, and Deuteronomist documents. For scholarly convenience each name was abbreviated to its first letter, so the documents are referred to more concisely as the J, E, P, and D documents. Once the interwoven documents were separated through critical Bible study, they revealed an ongoing tribal struggle between the Priesthoods descended from Moses (Mushites) and those from Aaron (Aaronids), and showed clearly how their struggles for power influenced both Israelite history and the writing of the Bible.

The J and E documents were written after the United Kingdom of David and Solomon had divided into the Southern Kingdom of Judah and the Northern Kingdom of Israel: J reflected the traditions of the Southern tribes (Rueben, Simeon, Levi, and Judah), and of the Aaronid priesthood serving at the Temple in Jerusalem; E reflected the traditions of the Northern tribes (Dan, Naphtali, Gad Asher, Issachar, Zebulon, Ephraim, Manasseh, Benjamin), and of the Mushite priesthood serving at the Tabernacle in Shiloh. The Tabernacle had been moved to Shiloh by Joshua following the conquest of Canaan, and remained there throughout the three-hundred-plus year period of the Judges.

J always refers to God as "Yahweh," while E refers to God as "Elohim" until his name is revealed to Moses as "Yahweh."

The J tradition emphasized Aaron's importance and subtlety diminished Moses', and maintained that only Levites descended from Aaron could be priests; the E tradition emphasized Moses' importance and diminished Aaron's, and maintained that *all* Levites could be priests. Both J and E traditions allowed sacrifice throughout the land.

When the Northern Kingdom was destroyed by Assyria, some surviving priests and Levites took refuge in the Southern Kingdom and brought with them the E document. At some time during the remaining life of the Southern Kingdom, an unknown editor merged the J and E documents to create a JE document that interwove the stories of both traditions almost seamlessly. The inclusion of nearly identical stories from both traditions resulted in many of the "doublets" found in the Bible – cases where the same story appears twice but with conflicting details.

It is unlikely that the Aaronid priests in the Southern Kingdom of Judah welcomed the introduction of texts that conflicted with their beliefs and doctrines. Their solution was to completely rewrite the JE document to their liking: they deliberately followed the JE order of events, but gave their own slant to the stories and added large bodies of priestly laws. They claimed that only Aaronids could be priests, and that sacrifices could only be offered at the Jerusalem Temple. This became the P, or Priestly source.

The final primary source includes most of the book of Deuteronomy, and so is called the Deuteronomist, or D source. It is part of a longer work, the "Deuteronomistic History," which extends from Deuteronomy through Joshua, Judges, 1&2 Samuel, and 1&2 Kings. Its viewpoint, like E, is also that of priests who were descendants of Moses (Mushites) and who had presided over the Tabernacle at the religious center of Shiloh. These later Mushite priests, like those who had earlier produced E, maintained that all Levites rather than just descendants of Aaron could be priests, and revered Moses rather than Aaron. They and their followers were undoubtedly incensed with the Aaronid priests rewriting of JE, so they responded by creating the D document by piecing together earlier texts and having the document, or a portion of it, "discovered" in the Temple at Jerusalem. They accepted that sacrifices could only be offered at the Tabernacle – now located at the Jerusalem Temple – but claimed that all Levites could be priests

These four sources were merged into their final form – the Five Books of Moses as we have them today – probably during the Second Temple period following the return from Exile. There is some evidence that this final redactor (sometimes referred to as "R") may have been Ezra, the exiled Aaronid priest-scribe who was charged by the Babylonian king to return to Jerusalem and teach and enforce "according to the law of your God which is in your hand." It, too, predictably, claimed that only Aaronids could be priests, and that sacrifices could only be offered at the (then being rebuilt) Jerusalem Temple.

This simplified overview of the primary sources does not do the Documentary Hypothesis justice, since it presents only the major conclusions without providing the overwhelming evidence supporting the conclusions. ... I recommend you read Richard Elliot Friedman's *"Who Wrote the Bible?"* or *"The Bible With Sources Revealed,"* to comprehend the magnitude and inexorable convergence of all the evidence.

Although details of the Documentary Hypothesis have been misused by anti-religious groups and individuals wanting to discredit Religion, the Hypothesis actually *strengthens* Judeo-Christianity by explaining heretofore puzzling Bible stories, providing an additional means of identifying teachings of Men ("the weeds") mingled with teachings of God ("the wheat"), and by allowing the true spiritual strength of "the wheat" to be recognized and revered.

The source documents, viewed separately, clearly reveal the continuous tribal struggles between the Aaronid and Mushite Priesthoods, and how their struggles affected Israelite history and the writing of the Bible. While all of Scripture is inspired by love of God and a desire to serve God faithfully, Man's tribal nature and allegiances have nonetheless allowed tribal prejudices to slip in and skew how God's truth is portrayed.

The time has come to begin conscientiously "separating the chaff from the wheat," and "refining the dross from the gold." The means of doing this is to *observe when teachings give power and authority to the groups proclaiming them and/or limit God's grace, goodness, or power to act.*

In the remainder of this chapter we will look for this primarily within Priestly groups; in the following two chapters we will look similarly at the Kings (and their courts) and the Prophets (and their guilds.)

How did the division between the Aaronid and Mushite priesthoods evolve? Did it begin during the Exodus, when the Hebrew priesthood originated? Did it begin in the early days in Canaan, when the tribes were allotted their territories and the Levites their cities? Did it begin during the ensuing three hundred or more years of the Judges, when priests offered sacrifices throughout the land? ... This can never be known, since the source documents weren't written until the priestly division had already hardened into mutual antagonism, and they were written by descendants (and beneficiaries) of the feuding factions who wanted to portray their current practices as being normative ever since the Exodus.

Being now aware of our tribal nature – our tendency to form tribes with differing beliefs and to impose them on others – it seems likely the priestly contentions existed in varying degrees throughout all this time before eventually reaching the polar opposition too often characteristic of human tribes. ... Think of how modern Liberals and Conservatives have progressed in fits and starts from mere disagreements to grid-lock enmity, with each side fervently blaming the other. ... Inevitably, our desire to increase the power and prestige of our tribe – and to strengthen its ability to impose our beliefs on others – overrides our objectivity and honesty and leads us down self-serving paths.

Is it likely that the God of the Universe – whom Prophets would later describe as caring about justice and mercy rather than feasts and holocausts – was concerned about which of the two priestly groups dominated? The Priestly claims clearly gave power and authority to themselves, and portrayed God as being more concerned with how and where He was worshipped and who led the worship rather than with whether Mankind "acted justly and loved mercy." Either of these conditions – the elevating of Man or the demeaning of God – should be a warning that a "teaching of Men," or "weeds among the wheat" is present.

Mushites initiate the United Kingdom

Despite the murkiness of their shared history, one thing is clear: the coming of the kingship improved the lot of the Aaronid priesthood and diminished that of the Mushites. Before the kingship the northern Mushite city of Shiloh was an Israelite center of worship that housed both the Tabernacle and the Ark of the Covenant for three hundred years. … Then came disaster.

 Foolishly treating the Ark as a magic-totem, the Israelite tribes carried it into battle against the Philistines only to lose heavily and have the Ark captured. The city of Shiloh was destroyed (presumably by the Philistines, although this is not recorded) but the Tabernacle was saved and moved to Gibeon, an Aaronid center of worship. The Ark was eventually returned by the Philistines (out of fear its presence was causing harm to their cities) and it was moved to the otherwise obscure town of Kiryat-Yearim where it was stored (apparently unused) for twenty years.

During that time Samuel, the first of the great Hebrew prophets, arose to become also the last of the great warrior-Judges, and led the Israelites to a decisive victory over the Philistines.

In Samuel's old age, however, the Israelite tribes asked Samuel to anoint a king over them. There are two versions of why they wanted a king; in one version it was because Samuel's sons and successors were corrupt and accepted bribes; in the other it was because they feared their tribal method of mustering troops was inadequate to oppose neighboring kings. Either way, under God's direction Samuel anointed Saul as the first king of a United Kingdom.

Mushites instigate the (first) breakup of the United Kingdom

There are also two versions of why Saul fell out of favor with God, leading Samuel to anoint David to succeed Saul, and eventually to the first breakup of the United Kingdom. In one version Saul didn't obey God's edict to destroy an enemy completely and take no booty; in the other he didn't obey Samuel's instruction to wait for him before offering a sacrifice. When Saul became aware that Samuel and the Shiloh priests now favored David, he ordered the Shiloh Mushite priests to be massacred: eighty-five priests were killed, and only one of the priests, Abiathar, escaped.

When Saul and his three oldest sons are killed in battle with the Philistines, the United Kingdom is no longer united: the tribe of Judah anoints David as their king, the Northern tribes anoint the remaining son of Saul, Ishbaal, as their king, and a long civil war ensues. The war ends when two of Isabaal's company commanders assassinate him; the elders of Israel go to David at Hebron and anoint him as king of Israel also, and once again there is a United Kingdom.

To consolidate his kingdom, David moves his capitol from Hebron to the more central Jerusalem, and appoints *two* chief priests, the Aaronid priest Zadok from Hebron, and the surviving Shiloh Mushite priest Abiathar. He also brought the Ark of the Covenant back from Kiryat-Yearim and had it installed in a tent he pitched for it in Jerusalem. (This tent was not the Tabernacle, which would remain in Gibeon until the reign of Solomon.) With both an Aaronid and a Mushite Chief Priest, the priesthood in Jerusalem probably had both Aaronid and Mushite priests, and perhaps even Levite priests not descended from Aaron or Moses; at this time, worship was not centralized in Jerusalem but was allowed throughout the land.

The Mushites lose power

When David became old there was infighting in the royal family over who would succeed him. The chief contenders were Adonijah (full brother of Absalom, who was killed in an earlier nearly-successful effort to overthrow David) and Solomon, son of David's favorite wife, Bathsheba. Adonijah had the advantage, for he was supported by the other princes, was well liked by the Northern tribes, and was supported by Joab, general of the tribal muster armies. Solomon was supported by the Southern tribes, by the general of the standing professional army, and by Nathan, the prophet who served as David's advisor and "conscience." ... The Aaronid Chief Priest Zadok supported Solomon, but the Mushite Chief Priest Abiathar supported Adonijah.

Nathan and Bathsheba conspired to inform David that Adonijah was publically acting as if he were already king, and to remind David he had promised Bathsheba that Solomon would be king. The intrigue worked, and David had Solomon anointed King, striking fear in Adonijah and those who supported him. Solomon allowed Adonijah to live ... until he made the mistake of asking for one of David's young consorts. Solomon then had Adonijah and Joab killed, and the Mushite Chief Priest Abiathar was deposed and exiled to the small Aaronid city of Anathoth, three miles from Jerusalem. Thereafter the Aaronids became and remained – with one significant exception – the dominant priesthood.

Despite not having a worship center or Chief Priest, the Shiloh Mushite priests nonetheless were able to exert their influence. Just as they had instigated the breakup of the first

United Kingdom by anointing and favoring David over Saul, they found a way to instigate a breakup of the second United Kingdom. ... But not without provocation.

Mushites instigate the final breakup of the United Kingdom

When Solomon succeeded David as King he began a massive building program, not only of the Temple (for which he is famously remembered) and his even larger palace, but also of military fortifications to defend Israel. To pay for this he ceded land containing twenty cities to Hiram, King of Tyre, created twelve administrative districts to each provide food for the Jerusalem court one month of the year, and established a "work tax" requiring citizens to work for the government one month of each year. ... But note: the cities given to Tyre were all Northern cities; the fortifications built were to defend Southern cities against Egypt rather than Northern cities against Assyria; and the Southern tribe of Judah was exempted from the administrative districts!

It was under these provoking conditions that Ahijah, a prophet associated with the Shiloh priesthood, approached Jeroboam, an Ephraimite leader of one of Solomon's work forces: Ahijah tore his cloak into twelve pieces representing the twelve tribes, and told Jeroboam that God was going to make him king over ten of the tribes. ... Jeroboam rebelled against Solomon, but was forced to flee to Egypt and remain there until Solomon died.

When Solomon's son Rehoboam assumed the throne, the Northern tribes asked that he lighten their burden; he replied by saying,

> "My father put on you a heavy yoke, but I will make it heavier.
> My father beat you with whips, but I will beat you with scorpions."
> (1 Kings 12:14)

It is no wonder they responded,

> "What share have we in David? We have no heritage in the
> son of Jesse. To your tents, O Israel! Now look to your own
> house, David."
> (1 Kings 12:16)

King Rehoboam sent his supervisor of forced labor to negotiate with the Northern leaders, but the supervisor was stoned to death and Israel was in full rebellion against Judah. Hearing this, the exiled Jeroboam returned from Egypt and was made king of Israel. Once again – this time permanently – the United Kingdom was divided, and once again the Mushite Shiloh priesthood had played a role in triggering the event.

Upon assuming the Northern throne, King Jeroboam had an immediate problem: his people worshipped Yahweh, but they had no Chief Priest, the Ark and Temple were in Jerusalem, and the Temple was overseen by Aaronid priests. Jeroboam's solution was to set up two new worship centers, one in Dan near the northern border, and one in Beth-El near the southern border with Judah; golden calves rather than winged cherubs were used to represent the presence of the invisible God.

It might be expected that in gratitude for the Shiloh priesthood anointing him king, King Jeroboam would appoint Mushite priests, or at least Levite priests, to serve at the worship centers. ... It was not to be. ... King Jeroboam cleverly decided to reduce the power of the priesthood in the Northern Kingdom by appointing anyone – even non-Levites – who would pay for the position: he and subsequent Northern kings would not have to contend with a powerful entrenched priesthood independent of the kings and courts. It is recorded in (Aaronid-biased) 2 Chronicles 11 that many Northern priests and Levites left their lands and holdings at this time to come to Judah and Jerusalem.

Shilonite and other non-Aaronid priests in both the North and the South now had no official position, power, or wealth ... but at least they could still serve at the "high places," the local shrines throughout the land. ... Or at least they could until the reign of Southern King Hezekiah.

The scholarly consensus is that sacrifices were permitted at local shrines throughout the land for about six hundred years (three hundred of Judges and three hundred of Kings) as described in the J and E documents. This dramatically changed during the reign of King Hezekiah, whose mother was the daughter of the Aaronid High Priest Zechariah. Early in Hezekiah's reign the Assyrians destroyed the Northern Kingdom and refugees began fleeing to the Southern Kingdom, bringing Mushite beliefs and doctrines with them.

The Aaronids strike back

Something had to be done to prevent these (false!) doctrines from spreading, and King Hezekiah arose to the challenge by proclaiming (probably with encouragement from the Aaronid priesthood) that sacrifices could be offered *only* by Aaronid priests and they could be offered *only* at the temple in Jerusalem. This was an unprecedented, devastating blow to the non-Aaronid priests throughout the land, for it took away their means of livelihood, of supporting their families.

It was at this time or shortly afterward that an Aaronid priest (or priests) wrote the P document, giving the impression that sacrifices had *never* been performed except by Aaronid priests, and that all other Levites, including Mushites, could only be assistants, never priests. To achieve this the P document had to deliberately omit all references to sacrifices by Cain, Abel, Noah, Abraham, Isaac, and Jacob, and had Noah take only *one* pair of "clean" animals on the ark since extra ones for sacrifice weren't needed.

Once again, the extreme self-promotion and the depiction of God as *authoring* this elevation of the descendants of Aaron and the diminishing of all other Levites should alert us to the presence of weeds among the wheat.

A Mushite resurgence?

The Mushite priesthood was also subject to tribal biases and equally susceptible to slanting history to their advantage when they had a chance to write it. Their opportunity came when Josiah – the great-grandson of King Hezekiah – became King.

It is not recorded how Shilonites came to have an influence within the court at this time, but apparently they did. It is possible that when the Mushite Chief Priest Abiathar was deposed and exiled to Anathoth, three miles from Jerusalem, other Mushite priests came with or followed him and a Shilonite enclave became established there. Strong hints of an Anathoth-Shiloh connection can be seen in the Book of Jeremiah, which opens with,

> "The words of Jeremiah, son of Hilkiah, of a priestly family in Anathoth."
> (Jeremiah 1:1)

In "*Who Wrote the Bible?*" Richard Elliot Freeman points out that Jeremiah is the only prophet who mentions Shiloh (he does so four times), and he refers to it identically as does Deuteronomy,

> "... the place where I (God) caused my name to dwell."
> (Jeremiah 7:12)

He is also the only prophet to refer to Samuel, the great Shilonite judge-priest, whom he almost equates with Moses:

> The Lord said to me: Even if Moses and Samuel stood before me, my heart would not turn toward this people.
> (Jeremiah 15:1)

Throughout the Book of Jeremiah there are many phrases that are word for word identical to phrases in Deuteronomy. Additionally, the Book of Jeremiah prominently mentions several public figures who are also mentioned in Second Kings. Second Kings records that while the Temple was being renovated, the High Priest *Hilkiah* discovered a scroll and gave it to the royal scribe, *Shaphan*, who took it to the King; the Book of Jeremiah records that Ahikam, *son of Shaphan*, saved Jeremiah from being stoned for prophesizing against Jerusalem, and that when Jerusalem fell the Babylon-appointed governor Gedaliah, son of Ahikam, *son of Shaphan* protected and provided for Jeremiah; when Jeremiah sent a letter to the exiles in Babylon it was delivered by Gemariah, *son of Hilkiah*, and Elasah, *son of Shaphan*. Jeremiah's life is clearly intertwined with those instrumental in disseminating the Temple document.

It is not known if Hilkiah "the father of Jeremiah" is also Hilkiah "the High Priest." … It is tempting to assume they were the same person, and some scholars do, but it is also possible they simply had the same name.

The scroll that Hilkiah found contained a law code and text that embodied the Mushite view of Israelite history: since only Aaronids were supposed to be priests at this time, it is puzzling that an Aaronid High Priest would have close associations with Shilonites and would participate in disseminating an essentially Mushite document. … Perhaps the restriction of the Jerusalem priesthood to Aaronids was not practiced as absolutely as the Priestly document claimed, just as Yahwist monotheism was often not practiced as absolutely as claimed. If so, it would allow the possibility that Hilkiah was Mushite, as his behavior and associations suggest.

Most scholars agree that the scroll found by Hilkiah contained some or all of the Deuteronomy portion of the D document, particularly the Deuteronomic law code. It is believed the D document was assembled from authentic older texts that were pieced together with connecting text, and – to give it authority – had an introduction and ending added that represented it as being the last testament of Moses. Because of the great similarities in viewpoint and phrasing between the D document and the book of Jeremiah, some scholars believe they were written by the same author, and that the author was probably Jeremiah's scribe, Baruch.

This powerful document motivated King Josiah to institute religious reforms in accordance with how the document described God's will for His People, and to embark on an effort to recapture all of the land given by God to his people, particularly the conquered Northern Kingdom. ... Again, it was not to be. ... While attempting to prevent an Egyptian army from passing through Judah to aid Assyria against Babylon, he was struck by an arrow and died at the early age of forty.

This catastrophic event undoubtedly devastated the Shilonite community, who saw Josiah as the God-given righter of all the wrongs that had been perpetrated against them over the centuries: Second Chronicles 35:25 records that Jeremiah composed a lamentation of Josiah's death. Several chapters were subsequently added to the D document so that it ended abruptly, not with Josiah's triumphs, but with the subjugation of Judah by Egypt, the destruction of Jerusalem by the Babylonians, the end of the Davidic dynasty ... and exile.

Once again, we see in the D document as well as the P document the willingness of the priestly tribes to rewrite history according to their own viewpoints and to their own benefit. Remember ...

- We compulsively form tribes and war with one another;
- We treat tribal beliefs as "territory" to be fiercely defended;
- We try to impose our tribal beliefs on other tribes;
- We make scapegoat enemies of tribes opposing our beliefs;
- We stereotype and caricature opposing tribes;
- We use law codes to impose our tribal beliefs;
- We use stories to pass on our tribal beliefs and culture.

And, once again, we should remind ourselves *this is characteristic human tribal behavior* not limited to ancient tribes

or to Jews, but easily discernible in all our modern tribes ... if we
have eyes to see.

As we look next at the histories of the kings and their courts
in the Hebrew Bible, we must keep in mind that the histories
were written by authors who were all priests or scribes (except
for the author of the J document) and whose viewpoints were
biased by their priestly tribe's beliefs.

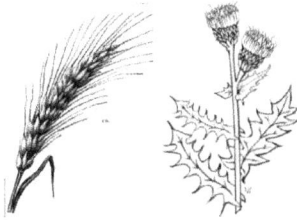

Chapter 4.
Kings and Courts

Kings are an enduring phenomenon in human history: whenever competing (warring) human tribes become large enough they seemingly instinctively switch from egalitarian leadership by the most proficient leader-warrior to a designated "king" with special rights and powers. A king is almost deliberately imbued with an aura of godliness by his subjects: they *want* him to have superhuman abilities to protect them and defeat their enemies, just as they want their god(s) to have those powers. Thus the elevation of a king or emperor to godlike status is not unusual, particularly since it's useful to the king's court ... those charged with implementing the king's will and whims, and keeping the populace supporting him.

Having the king or emperor viewed as a god vastly increases the power of the courts and courtiers, and kings and emperors usually accepted (or encouraged) this worshipful adulation since it validated their right to do anything they wanted. ... One notable exception to this was King Canute of England, Norway and Denmark, circa 1016-1035 C.E., who had his courtiers carry him to the seaside where he dramatically commanded the tide to turn back ... to prove to them that he did *not* possess such powers!

Hebrew kings, however, did not enjoy carte blanch to do as they pleased, since they were constrained by the priesthoods and prophets to be (nominally) subservient to God. The

Deuteronomic law code even contains a "Law of the King" which requires the king to be "chosen by God" (i.e., anointed by a prophet), limits the horses, wives, and wealth he can acquire, and requires him to have a copy of "the law which is in the custody of the Levite priests" and to read it "all the days of his life." (Deuteronomy 17: 14-18)

While Hebrew kings couldn't be considered to be gods, they had the next best thing: they were considered to be personally chosen and anointed by God. The Judean (Southern) kings had the added benefit that the linage of David had been designated by God to be kings of Judah/Israel in perpetuity:

> "Your house and your kingdom shall endure forever before me;
> your throne shall stand firm forever."
> (2 Samuel 7:16)

The covenant was made while David was king of the United Kingdom of both Judah and Israel, but after Israel broke away the covenant seems to have been tacitly reinterpreted to apply only to the kingdom of Judah.

Our knowledge of the Hebrew kings and their courts comes primarily from the historical books of Samuel, Kings, and Chronicles, and the prophetic books of First Isaiah and Jeremiah. All of these sources document the raw tribalism practiced by the Hebrew kings and their courts ... and reveal once again the biases of the priestly groups writing the histories.

Samuel and Kings are part of the Deuteronomist History written by Shilonite priests, and consequently reflect their view of Israelite history; Chronicles is part of the Chronicles-Ezra-Nehemiah document written by the Aaronid post-exilic redactor (who combined the J, E, P, D documents into their final form) and consequently reflects the Aaronid view of Israelite history.

The Book of Kings

The book of Kings provides a chronological summary of the reigns of all the Hebrew kings after David, alternating between Southern and Northern kings, and labeling each king as "good" (having pleased the Lord) or "bad" (having done evil in the sight of the Lord) depending upon their fidelity to Yahweh and to central worship in Jerusalem. Thus all the Northern kings were labeled as "bad" since they supported the golden calf shrines and impure priests at Dan and Beth-El. The Southern kings, descendants of David, were designated "good" or "bad" depending upon the degree to which they enforced worship of Yahweh and tore down the sacred poles and high places where other gods were worshipped. "Bad" kings, who tolerated or encouraged the high places and worship of other gods, would often be described as being like the Northern kings:

Jehoram ... conducted himself like the kings of Israel of the line of Ahab, since the sister of Ahab was his wife... and he did evil in the Lord's sight. Even so, the Lord was unwilling to destroy Judah, because of his servant David. For he had promised David that he would leave him a lamp in the Lord's presence for all time.
(2 Kings 8:18-19)

Ahaziah ... conducted himself like the house of Ahab, doing evil in the Lord's sight as they did, since he was related to them by marriage.
(2 Kings 8:27)

Ahaz ... did not please the Lord, his God, like his forefather David, but conducted himself like the kings of Israel, and even immolated his son by fire, in accordance with the abominable practice of the nations whom the Lord had cleared out of the way of the Israelites. Further, he sacrificed and burned incense on the high places, on hills, and under every leafy tree.
(2 Kings 16:2-4)

Manasseh ...did evil in the sight of the Lord, following the abominable practices of the nations whom the Lord had cleared out of the way of the Israelites. He rebuilt the high places which his father Hezekiah had destroyed. He erected altars to Baal, and also set up a sacred pole, as Ahab, king of Israel, had done.

He worshiped and served the whole host of heaven. He built altars in the temple of the Lord ... altars for the whole host of heaven, in the two courts of the temple. He immolated his son by fire. He practiced soothsaying and divination, and reintroduced the consulting of ghosts and spirits. He did much evil in the Lord's sight and provoked him to anger.
(2 Kings 21:2-6)

Amon ... did evil in the sight of the Lord, as his father Manasseh had done. He followed exactly the path his father had trod ... He abandoned the Lord, the God of his fathers, and did not follow the path of the Lord.
(2 Kings 21:20-22)

"Good" kings were praised as pleasing the Lord, but then it would often be noted that nonetheless they did not destroy the high places:

Asa ... pleased the Lord like his forefather David ... [but] The high places did not disappear.
(1 Kings 15:11-14)

Jehoshaphat ... followed all the ways of his father Asa unswervingly, doing what was right in the Lord's sight. Nevertheless, the high places did not disappear.
(1 Kings 22:43-44)

Joash did what was pleasing to the Lord as long as he lived ... Still, the high places did not disappear; the people continued to sacrifice and to burn incense there.
(2 Kings 12:3-4)

Amaziah ... pleased the Lord, yet not like his forefather David, since he did just as his father Joash had done. Thus the high places did not disappear, but the people continued to sacrifice and to burn incense on them.
(2 Kings 14:3-4)

Azariah pleased the Lord just as his father Amaziah had done. Yet the high places did not disappear; the people continued to sacrifice and to burn incense on them.
(2 Kings 15:3-4)

Jotham, ... pleased the Lord, just as his father Uzziah [Azariah] had done. Nevertheless the high places did not disappear and the people continued to sacrifice and to burn incense on them.
(2 Kings 15:32-35)

Only Hezekiah and Josiah, the two kings who *did* attempt to eliminate all the high places and impose centralized worship in Jerusalem were praised unstintingly. Of Hezekiah it was written:

> He put his trust in the Lord, the God of Israel; and neither before him nor after him was there anyone like him among all the kings of Judah.
> (2 Kings 18:5)

And of Josiah it was written:

> Before him there had been no king who turned to the Lord as he did, with his whole heart, his whole soul, and his whole strength, in accord with the entire law of Moses; nor could any after him compare with him.
> (2 Kings 23:25)

That these two citations seem unaware of each other is understandable when we remember that the Deuteronomist author incorporated portions of older, previously separate texts.

While both Hezekiah and Josiah are praised in the Book of Kings, Josiah is praised significantly more: where there is the equivalent of one paragraph describing Hezekiah's destruction of the high places, there is the equivalent of three paragraphs describing Josiah's, and in much greater detail. ... It records that Josiah defiled the high places set up east of Jerusalem by Solomon, which Hezekiah had apparently left untouched. For the Deuteronomist and the other priests of Shiloh, Josiah was the pinnacle of Davidic succession; his untimely death was a devastating disaster.

The Book of Chronicles

The Book of Chronicles also provides a summary of the Hebrew kings after David, but of *only the Southern kings*: it ignores the Northern kings except as necessary to describe the Southern kings' interactions with them. Most notably, it is known from extra-Biblical sources that Omri, father of Ahab, was one of the most important of the Northern kings. Omri made Samaria the Northern capital, conquered Moab, and formed alliances (strengthened by marriages) with both Tyre and Judah, ending the warfare between them; "Omri," and the "House of Omri," are mentioned prominently in archaeological records from both Moab and Assyria … yet in Chronicles Omri is mentioned only in genealogies, only in passing. (Kings at least mentions his making Samaria the Northern capital.)

The Chronicler used Kings as one of his sources – and often copied sections word for word – but he also incorporated other sources and introduced long narrative sections effusively praising the good kings and condemning the bad kings. These narrative sections differed from Kings in that they portrayed the Southern kings, particularly David, Solomon, and Hezekiah, as being intimately and enthusiastically involved in instituting the religious rituals and practices favored by the Aaronid priests; for the Chronicler, the kings' religious accomplishments were more important than their political and military accomplishments. For example, when David brought the Ark to Jerusalem Chronicles records:

> David built houses for himself in the City of David and prepared a place for the ark of God, pitching a tent for it there. At that time he said, "No one may carry the ark of God except the Levites, for the Lord chose them to carry the ark of the Lord and to minister to him forever."
> (1 Chron 15:1-2)

… In Kings there is no mention of this liturgical pronouncement by David, nor of the many others rituals enthusiastically reported by the Chronicler as being introduced by David, furthered by Solomon, and reinstated by Hezekiah. This shift of emphasis is understandable, since the Chronicler wrote following the Exile when Judaism was agonizingly accepting its demise as a significant nation militarily, and reinterpreting its importance as lying in its faithful worship of God at the rebuilt Temple in Jerusalem. Thus where the Book of Kings portrays kings favorably or unfavorably depending upon to what degree they supported Yahwist liturgical practices, the Book of Chronicles portrays favored kings as *instituting* those liturgical practices:

... for David's final orders were to enlist the Levites from the time they were twenty years old. David said: "The Lord, the God of Israel, has given rest to his people, and has taken up his dwelling in Jerusalem. Henceforth the Levites need not carry the Dwelling or any of its furnishings or equipment. Rather, their duty shall be to assist the sons of Aaron in the service of the house of the Lord, having charge of the courts, the chambers, and the preservation of everything holy: they shall take part in the service of the house of God. They shall also have charge of the showbread, of the fine flour for the cereal offering, of the wafers of unleavened bread, and of the baking and mixing, and of all measures of quantity and size. They must be present every morning to offer thanks and to praise the Lord, and likewise in the evening; and at every offering of holocausts to the Lord on sabbaths, new moons, and feast days, in such numbers as are prescribed, they must always be present before the Lord. They shall observe what is prescribed for them concerning the meeting tent, the sanctuary, and the sons of Aaron, their brethren, in the service of the house of the Lord."
(1 Chron 23:24-32)

... Then David gave to his son Solomon the pattern of the portico and of the building itself, with its storerooms, its upper rooms and inner chambers, and the room with the propitiatory. He provided also the pattern for all else that he had in mind by way of courts for the house of the Lord, with the surrounding compartments for the stores for the house of God and the stores of the votive offerings, as well as for the divisions of the priests and Levites, for all the work of the service of the house of the Lord, and for all the liturgical vessels of the house of the Lord. He specified the weight of gold to be used in the golden vessels for the various services and the weight of silver to be used in the silver vessels for the various services; likewise for the golden lampstands and their lamps he specified the weight of gold for each lampstand and its lamps, and for the silver lampstands he specified the weight of silver for each lampstand and its lamps, depending on the use to which each lampstand was to be put. He specified the weight of gold for each table to hold the showbread, and the silver for the silver tables; the pure gold to be used for the forks and pitchers; the amount of gold for each golden bowl and the silver for each silver bowl; the refined gold, and its weight, to be used for the altar of incense; and, finally, gold for what would suggest a chariot throne: the cherubim that spread their wings and covered the ark of the covenant of the Lord. He had

successfully committed to writing the exact specifications of the pattern, because the hand of the Lord was upon him.
(1 Chron 28:11-19)

... In those times Solomon offered holocausts to the Lord upon the altar of the Lord which he had built in front of the porch, as was required day by day according to the command of Moses, and in particular on the sabbaths, at the new moons, and on the fixed festivals three times a year: on the feast of the Unleavened Bread, the feast of Weeks and the feast of Booths. And according to the ordinance of his father David he appointed the various classes of the priests for their service, and the Levites according to their functions of praise and ministry alongside the priests, as the daily duty required. The gatekeepers of the various classes stood guard at each gate, since such was the command of David, the man of God. There was no deviation from the king's command in any respect relating to the priests and Levites or the treasuries. All of Solomon's work was carried out successfully from the day the foundation of the house of the Lord was laid until the house of the Lord had been completed in every detail.
(2 Chron 8:12-16)

Hezekiah ... in the first month of the first year of his reign, opened the doors of the Lord's house and repaired them. He summoned the priests and Levites, gathered them in the open space to the east, and said to them: "Listen to me, you Levites! Sanctify yourselves now and sanctify the house of the Lord, the God of your fathers, and clean out the filth from the sanctuary. ... My sons, be not negligent any longer, for it is you whom the Lord has chosen to stand before him, to minister to him, to be his ministers and to offer incense." Then the Levites arose: ... They gathered their brethren together and sanctified themselves; then they came as the king had ordered, to cleanse the Lord's house in keeping with his words. ... Then King Hezekiah ... went up to the Lord's house. Seven bulls, seven rams, seven lambs and seven he-goats were brought for a sin offering for the kingdom, for the sanctuary, and for Judah, and he ordered the sons of Aaron, the priests, to offer them on the altar of the Lord. ... He stationed the Levites in the Lord's house with cymbals, harps and lyres according to the prescriptions of David, of Gad the king's seer, and of Nathan the prophet; ... The entire assembly prostrated itself, and they continued to sing the song and to sound the trumpets until the holocaust had been completed. ...

They sang praises till their joy was full, then fell down and prostrated themselves. Hezekiah now spoke out this command: "You have undertaken a work for the Lord. Approach, and bring forward the sacrifices and thank offerings for the house of the Lord." Then the assembly brought forward the sacrifices and thank offerings and all the holocausts which were free-will offerings. ... Thus the service of the house of the Lord was reestablished. Hezekiah and all the people rejoiced over what God had reestablished for the people, and at how suddenly this had been done.
(2 Chron 29:1-36)

This exuberant enthusiasm contrasts sharply with the Book of Kings' versions of the same events, which simply describe the kings as dutifully performing established rituals. ... The Chronicler clearly strove to make the Aaronid view of proper worship be seen as the *only* proper worship, and to make it be seen as having been instituted and enforced, not by mere Aaronid priests, but by the great kings of Judah.

Regardless of the biases discernible in the biblical records of the Hebrew kings and their courts, the records clearly document the tribalism and tribal traits exhibited by them all: unvaryingly kings and courts engage in ongoing wars with rival nation-tribes, and in internal struggles with rival subtribes wanting to overthrow the king; the only periods of peace are when one of the nation-tribes dominates the others and imposes peace, or in the relatively few instances when treaties and royal intermarriages succeed in procuring temporary peace. Biblical history, alongside secular history, accurately portrays Man as continually forming tribes, warring with one another, and trying to impose their tribal beliefs (especially belief in their gods) on one another: it shows tribes compulsively killing and dying for beliefs as fiercely as for territory, of scapegoating, caricaturing, and demeaning rival tribes, and of crying, "Peace, peace," while waging War, war.

Accepting the Bible's portrayal of Man as a tribal territorial animal, whose tribes are based on shared tribal beliefs and who compulsively contend to impose their tribal beliefs on others, is a necessary first step toward developing a successful stratagem to counter our predisposition to war. ... Until we fully accept that unconscious instincts bias our conscious thinking and distort how we view one another, we will be incapable of ever overcoming our biases and living in peace. As we will see in Part 2, the teachings of Jesus directly confront and challenge our negative tribal traits.

The Biblical history of almost any of the Hebrew monarchs could be used to illustrate archetypical tribal behavior, but one reign is particularly illustrative because it also demonstrates our tendency to ignore data contrary to existing beliefs. ... The belief that there would always be a descendent of David on the throne of Judah is so powerful that we seldom acknowledge – and certainly don't emphasize – that for six years not only was there not a king descended from David on the throne of Judah, but instead there was a queen descended from Jezebel!

The Biblical story of Queen Athaliah of Judah is so bizarre that it reads like a soap opera, but so powerful and intriguing that George Frederick Handel composed an oratorio, *Athalia*, based upon it. The story is recorded in both Kings and Chronicles: in Kings it is told in snippets interspersed with the Elijah and Elisha cycles, so it is understandable that its significance could be overlooked; in Chronicles, however, it is told uninterrupted from beginning to end, making it plain that the Davidic dynasty was indeed interrupted by the six years of Athaliah's reign. ... This exception is seldom mentioned whenever the *"There will always be a descendent of David on the throne"* theme is reiterated ... showing once again that we are predisposed to ignore facts conflicting with existing beliefs.

The Queen Athaliah saga began in what was the most prosperous time for Israel and Judah since the final breakup of the United Kingdom: the Northern Kingdom had won back territory that had been lost to Moab, the Southern Kingdom had won back territory that had been lost to Edom, and for the first time since their separation Israel and Judah controlled nearly as much land as in the time of David and Solomon. King Ahab of

Israel and King Jehoshaphat of Judah were allies, and strengthened their relationship through the marriage of Ahab's (and Jezebel's) daughter, Athaliah, to Jehoshaphat's son, Jehoram.

The prosperity did not last.

In the Northern Kingdom, Ahab died and his son Ahaziah became king, but Queen Mother Jezebel was the power behind the throne. Ahaziah was doomed to a short reign, falling from a roof garden and dying from injuries. Ahab and Jezebel's second son, Jehoram, succeeded Ahaziah as king, and Jezebel remained in power as Queen Mother.

In the Southern Kingdom, Jehoshaphat died and his son (also named Jehoram) became king, thus making his wife, Athaliah – the daughter of Jezebel – queen of Judah. Their children included an oldest son named Ahaziah (after his uncle, the Northern king who had fallen and died), and a daughter named Jehosheba, who becomes the heroine of the saga. After a reign of only eight years, during which time Edom was lost, King Jehoram of Judah died a painful death from a bowel disease and his oldest son, Ahaziah, was anointed king of Judah; Queen Mother Athaliah, like her mother Jezebel in Israel, remained the power behind the throne.

Then came incredible tragedy: the kings of Judah and Israel were both killed on the same day, by the same man.

The ongoing warfare between the priests of Baal (aided by Jezebel) and the priests of Yahweh (aided by Elijah) resulted in followers of Elijah anointing Jehu, a general in the Northern army, to revolt against Jezebel and her son, King Jehoram. Judah's King Ahaziah happened to be visiting King Jehoram when Jehu and a troop of his soldiers arrived; they killed King Jehoram with an arrow through the heart, and wounded King Ahaziah. Ahaziah escaped, but died from his wound shortly afterward. … Jehu proceeded on to have Jezebel killed at Jezreel, and began establishing his own dynasty by ordering the killing of all the descendants of Ahab.

With Judah's King Ahaziah dead, his oldest son should have become king. Instead, Queen Athaliah gave the phrase, "daughter of Jezebel", a truly terrifying meaning: she seized power and began to kill off the entire royal family ... including her own grandchildren. ... Had she succeeded completely, the Davidic dynasty would have come to a very premature end. She was foiled by her own daughter, Jehosheba – sister of Ahaziah, and wife of the high priest Jehoiada – who hid Ahaziah's infant son, Joash, in the temple precincts for six years while Athaliah reigned. In the seventh year Jehoiada conspired with others to bring young Joash out and, with great fanfare, to anoint him king. ... When Athaliah came to see the reason for the commotion, she was dragged away and unceremoniously slain, finally ending the interruption of the Davidic kingship.

The monarchy of Athalia is particularly soap-operaesque, but the other Hebrew monarchies also demonstrate typical human tribal faults. The impulse of a successor to the throne to eliminate potential rivals by killing them, even when they're young children or adolescents, appalls our sensitivities and tarnishes our image of humanity. ... While we accept that many other mammals kill their young under particular circumstances – usually ascendant males killing the offspring of their predecessors – we really don't want to accept that it might be unconscious instincts driving us to similar actions. Nonetheless, it is recorded ...

> Nadab, son of Jeroboam, became king of Israel ... Baasha, son of Ahijah, killed him and reigned in his stead. Once he was king, he killed off the entire house of Jeroboam, not leaving a single soul to Jeroboam but destroying him utterly ...
> (1 King 15:25-30)

> Elah, son of Baasha, began his two-year reign over Israel ... His servant Zimri ... plotted against him. As he was ... drinking to excess ...Zimri entered; he struck and killed him ... and reigned in his place. Once he was seated on the royal throne, he killed off the whole house of Baasha, not sparing a single male relative or friend of his.
> (1 Kings 16:8-11)

When we read that lactating female prairie dogs sometimes invade the nests of other females to kill, and even eat their brood, we shudder but accept it. When we read of Athaliah's willingness to callously kill her own grandchildren we shudder, but resist accepting it as a tribal instinct to further her own tribal interests. The reality is that we will never be able to understand – let alone lessen – the negative effects of our tribal instincts unless and until we acknowledge they exist and influence our behavior: a useful aphorism (stated in *Man by Nature*) is, "*Once you realize Man is not rational, things begin to make sense.*"

Throughout all the Biblical histories of the kings and their courts, it can be seen once again that:

- We compulsively form tribes and war with one another;
- We treat tribal beliefs as "territory" to be fiercely defended;
- We try to impose our tribal beliefs on other tribes;
- We make scapegoat enemies of tribes opposing our beliefs;
- We stereotype and caricature opposing tribes;
- We use law codes to impose our tribal beliefs;
- We use stories to pass on our tribal beliefs and culture.

❦

We've now considered the Priests and the Kings, two of the three major hierarchies governing in the ancient Middle East. We turn now to the third, and most enigmatic … the Prophets.

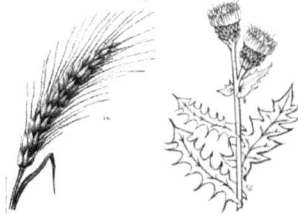

Chapter 5.
Prophets and Spokesmen

The Hebrew Prophets bring fresh, God-breathed air to the Bible. While the Priests and Kings served God, their service was adulterated by their tribal interests: the Priests dictated the feasts, holocausts, and rituals they believed were important to Yahweh (and coincidentally gave them position, wealth, and power) and the Kings enforced those dictates to whatever degree suited them, often intermixing them with the worship of other gods. Neither the Priests nor the Kings questioned whether the way they worshipped Yahweh was what God wanted, and their consequent venal behavior earned much of the criticism directed at historical Judaism.

The Prophets did question ... and accuse. They accused the Priests, the Kings, the Princes, the leaders, and the people of the land of not being faithful to God's wishes: they proclaimed in many, often flamboyant ways that:

- The nation is morally corrupt: it does not obey God;
- The nation's leaders allow social injustice;
- Disaster will befall the nation unless it repents;
- False priests and prophets lead the people astray;

- Worshipping man-made idols or other gods is foolish and abominable;
- The "Day of the Lord" will bring judgment, not reward;
- God uses other nations to punish Israel;
- A faithful remnant will survive;
- God will someday create a New Jerusalem, a perfect society;
- God is god of all the nations, not just Israel;
- All nations will eventually turn to the God of Zion;
- Individuals are responsible only for their own sins, not "sons for the sins of their fathers";
- "Teachings of men" distort God's will for Man;
- God wants caring for others, not religious rituals.

While no individual Prophet emphasized all of these themes (which have been distilled from all of their writings) together their voices form a "mighty chorus" proclaiming the Will of God to recalcitrant Man. … Some representative examples of these themes are:

The nation is morally corrupt: it does not obey God

Hear the word of the Lord, O people of Israel, for the Lord has a grievance against the inhabitants of the land: there is no fidelity, no mercy, no knowledge of God in the land. False swearing, lying, murder, stealing and adultery! In their lawlessness, bloodshed follows bloodshed.
(Hosea 4:1-2)

The nation's leaders allow social injustice

Woe to those who enact unjust statutes and who write oppressive decrees, depriving the needy of judgment and robbing my poor people of their rights, making widows their plunder, and orphans their prey!
(Isaiah 10:1-2)

Disaster will befall the nation unless it repents

Therefore this is what the Sovereign LORD says: "An enemy will overrun the land; he will pull down your strongholds and plunder your fortresses." This is what the LORD says: "As a shepherd saves from the lion's mouth only two leg bones or a piece of an ear, so will the Israelites be saved, those who sit in Samaria on the edge of their beds and in Damascus on their couches."
(Amos 3:11-12)

False priests and prophets lead the people astray

Hear this, you leaders of the house of Jacob, you rulers of the house of Israel, who despise justice and distort all that is right; who build Zion with bloodshed, and Jerusalem with wickedness. Her leaders judge for a bribe, her priests teach for a price, and her prophets tell fortunes for money. Yet they lean upon the LORD and say, "Is not the LORD among us? No disaster will come upon us."
(Micah 3:9-11)

Worshipping man-made idols or other gods is foolish and abominable

With their silver and gold they made idols for themselves, to their own destruction. Cast away your calf, O Samaria! my wrath is kindled against them; how long will they be unable to attain innocence in Israel? The work of an artisan no god at all, destined for the flames --- such is the calf of Samaria! When they sow the wind, they shall reap the whirlwind.
(Hosea 8:4b-7)

The "Day of the Lord" will bring judgment, not reward;

Woe to those who yearn for the day of the Lord! What will this day of the Lord mean for you? Darkness and not light! As if a man went to flee from a lion, and a bear should meet him; ... Will not the day of the Lord be darkness and not light, gloom without any brightness?
(Amos 5:18-20)

God uses other nations to punish Israel
He will give a signal to a far-off nation, and whistle to them from the ends of the earth; speedily and promptly will they come. None of them will stumble with weariness, none will slumber and none will sleep. None will have his waist belt loose, nor the thong of his sandal broken. Their arrows are sharp, and all their bows are bent. The hoofs of their horses seem like flint, and their chariot wheels like the hurricane.
(Isaiah 5:26-28)

A faithful remnant will survive
On that day the remnant of Israel, the survivors of the house of Jacob, will no more lean upon him who struck them; but they will lean upon the Lord, the Holy One of Israel, in truth. A remnant will return, the remnant of Jacob, to the mighty God.
(Isaiah 10:20-21)

God will someday create a New Jerusalem, a perfect society
Lo, I am about to create new heavens and a new earth; The things of the past shall not be remembered or come to mind. Instead, here shall always be rejoicing and happiness in what I create; For I create Jerusalem to be a joy and its people to be a delight; I will rejoice in Jerusalem and exult in my people. No longer shall the sound of weeping be heard there, or the sound of crying …
(Isaiah 65:17-19)

God is god of all the nations, not just Israel
"Are you not like Ethiopians to me, O men of Israel, says the Lord? Did I not bring the Israelites from the land of Egypt as I brought the Philistines from Caphtor and the Arameans from Kir?"
(Amos 9:7)

All nations will eventually turn to the God of Zion
Many nations will come and say, "Come, let us go up to the mountain of the LORD, to the house of the God of Jacob. He will teach us his ways, so that we may walk in his paths." The law will go out from Zion, the word of the LORD from Jerusalem. He will judge between many peoples and will settle disputes for strong nations far and wide. They will beat their swords into plowshares and their spears into pruning hooks. Nation will not take up sword against nation, nor will they train for war anymore.
(Micah 4:2-3)

Individuals are responsible only for their own sins, not "sons for the sins of their fathers"

What is the meaning of this proverb that you recite in the land of Israel: "Fathers have eaten green grapes, thus their children's teeth are on edge"? As I live, says the Lord God: I swear that there shall no longer be anyone among you who will repeat this proverb in Israel. For all lives are mine; the life of the father is like the life of the son, both are mine; only the one who sins shall die.

(Ezekiel 18:2-4)

"Teachings of men" distort God's will for Man

The Lord said: "Since this people draws near with words only and honors me with their lips alone, though their hearts are far from me, and their reverence for me has become routine observance of the precepts of men, therefore I will again deal with this people in surprising and wondrous fashion; the wisdom of its wise men shall perish and the understanding of its prudent men be hid.".

(Isaiah 29:13-14)

God wants caring for others, not religious rituals

I hate, I spurn your feasts, I take no pleasure in your solemnities; your cereal offerings I will not accept, nor consider your stall-fed peace offerings. Away with your noisy songs! I will not listen to the melodies of your harps. But if you would offer me holocausts, then let justice surge like water, and goodness like an unfailing stream.

(Amos 5:21-24)

Although it has become common to refer to *all* the Prophets as "Spokesmen for God," that description accurately applies only to those seeking to *reform* Yahwehism to reflect God's will. ... Some of the prophets were spokesmen for *Israel* (hurling oracles against other nations) or spokesmen for *Yahwehism* (exhorting faithful practice of Yahwehism and railing against worshipping other gods) but accepting the teachings and rituals of the Yahwist priesthood as being God ordained. ... Only the "Reform Prophets" – those who sought to *reform* Yahwist religious practices – deserve the designation, "Spokesmen for God."

The Reform Prophets burst onto the scene with the suddenness of a blast from a ram's horn, about 200 years after the reign of David and 150 years after his kingdom divided. Within a short sixty-year span, they and their followers introduced seeds of thought that would flower into the Deuteronomic reformation. Those sixty years encompassed the total destruction and exile of the Northern Kingdom and the devastation of the Southern Kingdom. It is believed that the writing of the book of Deuteronomy and the shaping of the books of Judges, Samuel, and Kings took place following this time, and that those writings were influenced by the Reform Prophets' teachings. When the scroll of Deuteronomy was "discovered" in the Jerusalem temple during King Josiah's reign, it sparked a sweeping and irreversible change in Judaism.

Who were these "Reform Prophets"? ... They were Amos, Hosea, First Isaiah, and Micah – the first of the "Writing Prophets," as the Prophets having a book of the Bible named after them are known. The tables on the following page show where they appear in the Hebrew Bible, and where they appeared chronologically in history.

The "Representative Quotes" in the chronological table show that the Reform Prophets took the radical point of view that God neither needed nor wanted religious rituals, but simply wanted Man to be good and to do good: they essentially equated true worship, true religion, with social justice. They disagreed with and criticized as "false prophets" the court prophets who worked for the king and provided oracles favorable to him. Their teachings repeatedly emphasized the radical view that:

- Love for fellowman is equivalent to love for God;

- Religious observances not arising from an underlying love of God and fellowman are meaningless.

Where the Reform Prophets Appear in the Hebrew Bible

Former Prophets	Latter Prophets	The Twelve	
Joshua	*Isaiah*	**Hosea**	Nahum
Judges	Jeremiah	Joel	Habakkuk
Samuel	Ezekiel	*Amos*	Zephaniah
Kings (Elijah & Elisha)		Obadiah	Haggai
		Jonah	Zechariah
		Micah	Malachi

Where the Reform Prophets Appear Chronologically

Prophet	B.C.E.	Representative Quote
Amos	≈760-746	"But if you would offer me holocausts, then let justice surge like water, and goodness like an unfailing stream." (Amos 5:23-24)
Hosea	≈745-724	"For it is love that I desire, not sacrifice, and knowledge of God rather than holocausts." (Hosea 6:6)
First Isaiah (Chaps 1-39 Less 24-27)	≈742-700	"Stop doing wrong, learn to do right! Seek justice, encourage the oppressed. Defend the cause of the fatherless, plead the case of the widow." (Isaiah 1:16b-17)
Micah	≈727-701	"He has showed you, O man, what is good. And what does the LORD require of you? To act justly and to love mercy and to walk humbly with your God." (Micah 6:8)

While not stated explicitly, the implication of these intertwined themes is that true religion is measured by the inner attitudes that result in outer actions rather than the by the outer actions themselves. … They did not call for the abandonment of religious rituals, but rather for the recognition that the rituals are meaningless unless accompanied and motivated by love of God and their fellowman.

Generations later, Jeremiah, Third Isaiah, and Malachi also cried out for religious reform, echoing the teachings of the trailblazing eighth century B.C.E. Reform Prophets. While the exile prophet Ezekiel also railed against "false prophets" and corrupt "princes of Israel," he called only for the faithful practice of Yahwehism, not its reform; similarly the Former Prophets, especially Elijah and Elisha, were spokesmen for Yahwehism, but not for its reform.

Where the Later Reform Prophets Appear Chronologically

Prophet	B.C.E.	Representative Quote
Jeremiah	≈627-575	... "if you do not oppress the alien, the fatherless or the widow and do not shed innocent blood in this place, and if you do not follow other gods ... then I will let you live in this place, in the land I gave your forefathers for ever and ever." (Jeremiah 7:6-7)
Third Isaiah (Chaps 56-66)	≈530?	"Is not this the kind of fasting I have chosen: to loose the chains of injustice and untie the cords of the yoke, to set the oppressed free and break every yoke?" (Isaiah 58:6)
Malachi	≈500-450	"I will draw near to you for judgment, and I will be swift to bear witness against sorcerers, adulterers, and perjurers, those who defraud the hired man of his wages, against those who defraud widows and orphans; those who turn aside the stranger, and those who do not fear me, says the Lord of hosts. (Malachi 3:5)

To illustrate the (now seven) Reform Prophets impassioned, relentless insistence that love for fellowman is equivalent to love of God, and that religious observances not arising from a love of God and fellowman are meaningless, consider these expanded and additional quotes:

Amos

Thus says the Lord: For three crimes of Judah, and for four, I will not revoke my word; Because they spurned the law of the Lord, and did not keep his statutes; Because the lies which their fathers followed have led them astray, I will send fire upon Judah, to devour the castles of Jerusalem. Thus says the Lord: For three crimes of Israel, and for four, I will not revoke my word; Because they sell the just man for silver, and the poor man for a pair of sandals. They trample the heads of the weak into the dust

of the earth, and force the lowly out of the way. Son and father go to the same prostitute, profaning my holy name. Upon garments taken in pledge they recline beside any altar; And the wine of those who have been fined they drink in the house of their god.
(Amos 2:4-8)

Come to Bethel and sin, to Gilgal, and sin the more; Each morning bring your sacrifices, every third day, your tithes; Burn leavened food as a thanksgiving sacrifice, proclaim publicly your freewill offerings, for so you love to do, O men of Israel, says the Lord GOD. Though I have made your teeth clean of food in all your cities, and have made bread scarce in all your dwellings, Yet you returned not to me, says the Lord.
(Amos 4:4-6)

Woe, to those who turn judgment into wormwood and cast justice to the ground!
(Amos 5:7)

Seek good and not evil, that you may live; ... Hate evil and love good, and let justice prevail at the gate;
(Amos 5:14-15a)

I hate, I spurn your feasts, I take no pleasure in your solemnities; your cereal offerings I will not accept, nor consider your stall-fed peace offerings. Away with your noisy songs! I will not listen to the melodies of your harps. But if you would offer me holocausts, then let justice surge like water, and goodness like an unfailing stream.
(Amos 5:21-24)

Yet you have turned judgment into gall, and the fruit of justice into wormwood.
(Amos 6:12b)

Hosea

Hear the word of the Lord, O people of Israel, for the Lord has a grievance against the inhabitants of the land: there is no fidelity, no mercy, no knowledge of God in the land. False swearing, lying, murder, stealing and adultery! In their lawlessness, bloodshed follows bloodshed.
(Hosea 4:1-2)

"With you is my grievance, O priests! You shall stumble in the day, and the prophets shall stumble with you at night; ... my people perish for want of knowledge! Since you have rejected knowledge, I will reject you from my priesthood.
(Hosea 4:4b-6a)

The more the priests increased, the more they sinned against me; they exchanged their Glory for something disgraceful. They feed on the sins of my people and relish their wickedness. And it will be: Like people, like priests. I will punish both of them for their ways and repay them for their deeds.
(Hosea 4:7-9)

What can I do with you, Ephraim? What can I do with you, Judah? Your piety is like a morning cloud, like dew that early passes away. For this reason I smote them through the prophets, I slew them by the words of my mouth; For it is love that I desire, not sacrifice, and knowledge of God rather than holocausts.
(Hosea 6:4-6)

They made kings, but not by my authority; they established princes, but without my approval With their silver and gold they make idols for themselves to their own destruction. Throw out your calf-idol, O Samaria! My anger burns against them. How long will they be incapable of purity? They are from Israel! This calf --a craftsman has made it; it is not God. It will be broken in pieces, that calf of Samaria.
(Hosea 8:4-6)

First Isaiah

"The multitude of your sacrifices -- what are they to me?" says the LORD. "I have more than enough of burnt offerings, of rams and the fat of fattened animals; I have no pleasure in the blood of bulls and lambs and goats. When you come to appear before me, who has asked this of you, this trampling of my courts? Stop bringing meaningless offerings! Your incense is detestable to me. New Moons, Sabbaths and convocations-- I cannot bear your evil assemblies. Your New Moon festivals and your appointed feasts my soul hates. They have become a burden to me; I am weary of bearing them. When you spread out your hands in prayer, I will hide my eyes from you; even if you offer many prayers, I will not listen. Your hands are full of blood; wash and make yourselves clean. Take your evil deeds out of my sight! Stop doing wrong, learn to do right! Seek justice,

encourage the oppressed. Defend the cause of the fatherless, plead the case of the widow.
(Isaiah 1:11-17)

How has she turned adulterous, the faithful city, so upright! Justice used to lodge within her, but now, murderers. Your silver is turned to dross, your wine is mixed with water, your princes are rebels and comrades of thieves; each of them loves a bribe and looks for gifts. The fatherless they defend not, and the widow's plea does not reach them.
(Isaiah 1:21-23)

Woe to you who join house to house, who connect field to field, till no room remains, and you are left to dwell alone in the midst of the land!
(Isaiah 5:8)

Woe to those who call evil good, and good evil, who change darkness into light, and light into darkness, who change bitter into sweet, and sweet into bitter! Woe to those who are wise in their own sight, and prudent in their own esteem! The valiant at mixing strong drink! Woe to the champions at drinking wine, to those who acquit the guilty for bribes, and deprive the just man of his rights!
(Isaiah 5:20-23)

Woe to those who enact unjust statutes and who write oppressive decrees, depriving the needy of judgment and robbing my poor people of their rights, making widows their plunder, and orphans their prey!
(Isaiah 10:1-2)

The Lord said: "Since this people draws near with words only and honors me with their lips alone, though their hearts are far from me, and their reverence for me has become routine observance of the precepts of men, therefore I will again deal with this people in surprising and wondrous fashion; the wisdom of its wise men shall perish and the understanding of its prudent men be hid."
(Isaiah 29:13-14)

Micah

Woe to those who plan iniquity, to those who plot evil on their beds! At morning's light they carry it out because it is in their power to do it. They covet fields and seize them, and houses, and take them. They defraud a man of his home, a fellowman of his inheritance.
(Micah 2:1-2)

Then I said, "Listen, you leaders of Jacob, you rulers of the house of Israel. Should you not know justice, you who hate good and love evil; who tear the skin from my people and the flesh from their bones; who eat my people's flesh, strip off their skin and break their bones in pieces; who chop them up like meat for the pan, like flesh for the pot?"
(Micah 3:1-3)

With what shall I come before the LORD and bow down before the exalted God? Shall I come before him with burnt offerings, with calves a year old? Will the LORD be pleased with thousands of rams, with ten thousand rivers of oil? Shall I offer my firstborn for my transgression, the fruit of my body for the sin of my soul? He has showed you, O man, what is good. And what does the LORD require of you? To act justly and to love mercy and to walk humbly with your God.
(Micah 6:6-8)

Am I still to forget, O wicked house, your ill-gotten treasures and the short ephah, which is accursed? Shall I acquit a man with dishonest scales, with a bag of false weights? Her rich men are violent; her people are liars and their tongues speak deceitfully.
(Micah 6:10-12)

The godly have been swept from the land; not one upright man remains. All men lie in wait to shed blood; each hunts his brother with a net. Both hands are skilled in doing evil; the ruler demands gifts, the judge accepts bribes, the powerful dictate what they desire-- they all conspire together. The best of them is like a brier, the most upright worse than a thorn hedge. The day of your watchmen has come, the day God visits you. Now is the time of their confusion. '
(Micah 7:2-4)

Jeremiah

For there are among my people criminals; like fowlers they set traps, but it is men they catch. Their houses are as full of treachery as a bird-cage is of birds; therefore they grow powerful and rich, fat and sleek. They go their wicked way; justice they do not defend by advancing the claims of the fatherless or judging the cause of the poor.
(Jeremiah 5:26-28)

The prophets prophesy falsely, and the priests teach as they wish.
(Jeremiah 5:31)

Small and great alike, all are greedy for gain; prophet and priest, all practice fraud. They would repair, as though it were naught, the injury to my people: "Peace, peace!" they say, though there is no peace. They are odious; they have done abominable things, yet they are not ashamed, they know not how to blush. Hence they shall be among those who fall; in their time of punishment they shall go down, says the Lord.
(Jeremiah 6:13-15)

This is what the LORD Almighty, the God of Israel, says: Reform your ways and your actions, and I will let you live in this place. Do not trust in deceptive words and say, "This is the temple of the LORD, the temple of the LORD, the temple of the LORD!" If you really change your ways and your actions and deal with each other justly, if you do not oppress the alien, the fatherless or the widow and do not shed innocent blood in this place, and if you do not follow other gods to your own harm, then I will let you live in this place, in the land I gave your forefathers for ever and ever.
(Jeremiah 7:3-7)

How can you say, "We are wise, we have the law of the Lord"? Why that has been changed into falsehood by the lying pen of the scribes!
(Jeremiah 8:8)

Both prophet and priest are godless! In my very house I find their wickedness, says the Lord. ... Among Samaria's prophets I saw unseemly deeds ... among Jerusalem's prophets I saw deeds still more shocking: adultery, living in lies, siding with the wicked, so that no one turns from evil; to me they are all like Sodom, its citizens like Gomorrah.
(Jeremiah 23:11-14)

Therefore I am against the prophets, says the Lord, who steal my words from each other. Yes, I am against the prophets, says the Lord, who borrow speeches to pronounce oracles. Yes, I am against the prophets who prophesy lying dreams, says the Lord, and who lead my people astray by recounting their lies and by their empty boasting. From me they have no mission or command, and they do this people no good at all, says the Lord.
(Jeremiah 23:30-32)

Third Isaiah

Is not this the kind of fasting I have chosen: to loose the chains of injustice and untie the cords of the yoke, to set the oppressed free and break every yoke? Is it not to share your food with the

hungry and to provide the poor wanderer with shelter-- when you see the naked, to clothe him, and not to turn away from your own flesh and blood?
(Isaiah 58:6-7)

Then you will call, and the LORD will answer; you will cry for help, and he will say: Here am I. "If you do away with the yoke of oppression, with the pointing finger and malicious talk, and if you spend yourselves in behalf of the hungry and satisfy the needs of the oppressed, then your light will rise in the darkness, and your night will become like the noonday.
(Isaiah 58:9-10)

The Spirit of the Sovereign LORD is on me, because the LORD has anointed me to preach good news to the poor. He has sent me to bind up the brokenhearted, to proclaim freedom for the captives and release from darkness for the prisoners, to proclaim the year of the Lord's favor and the day of vengeance of our God, to comfort all who mourn, and provide for those who grieve in Zion -- to bestow on them a crown of beauty instead of ashes, the oil of gladness instead of mourning, and a garment of praise instead of a spirit of despair.
(Isaiah 61:1-3a)

Malachi

For the lips of the priests are to keep knowledge, and instruction is to be sought from his mouth, because he is the messenger of the Lord of hosts. But you have turned aside from the way, and have caused many to falter by your instruction; you have made void the covenant of Levi, says the Lord of hosts. I, therefore have made you contemptible and base before all the people, since you do not keep my ways, but show partiality in your decisions.
(Malachi 2:7-9)

This also you do: the alter of the Lord you cover with tears, weeping and groaning, because he no longer regards your sacrifice nor accepts it favorably from your hand.
(Malachi 2:13)

You have wearied the Lord with your words, yet you say, "How have we wearied him?" By your saying, "Every evildoer is good in the sight of the Lord, and he is pleased with him"; or else, "Where is the just God?"
(Malachi 2:17)

Lo, I am sending my messenger to prepare the way for me; and suddenly there will come to the temple the Lord whom you seek,

and the messenger of the covenant whom you desire. Yes, he is coming, says the Lord of hosts. But who will endure the day of his coming? And who can stand when he appears?
(Malachi 3:1-2a)

I will draw near to you for judgment, and I will be swift to bear witness against sorcerers, adulterers, and perjurers, those who defraud the hired man of his wages, against those who defraud widows and orphans; those who turn aside the stranger, and those who do not fear me, says the Lord of hosts.
(Malachi 3:5)

⟢⟣

It could be argued that the power struggle between the Reform Prophets and the Priests and Court Prophets is a struggle between whether God is "Transcendent" or "Tribal," or even that it is a manifestation of the eternal struggle between "*the Spirit*" and "*the Flesh*." … Either way, once the Reform Prophets introduced the notion that God was Good and Goodness and wanted his people – all people – to also be good and caring, the battle was joined, and continues. … Does God care more for the doctrines and sacraments that divide us, or for the loving, caring, and forgiveness that binds us? … The Reform Prophets clearly, unequivocally, and outspokenly declared the latter.

⟢⟣

There are other themes tantalizingly touched on by the Reform Prophets but not developed: they rejected the "jealous God" theology; they did not view the scripture existent at their time as inerrant; and they hinted that God may care for all the nations, not just Israel.

On the Jealous God Theology

It is well remembered that when God gave Moses the Ten Commandments he described himself as:

For I, the Lord, your God, am a jealous God, inflicting punishment for their fathers' wickedness on the children of those who hate me, down to the third and fourth generation; but bestowing mercy down to the thousandth generation, on the children of those who love me and keep my commandments.
(Exodus 20 and Deuteronomy 5)

It is equally well remembered that when God was giving Moses a second set of tablets to replace the broken ones (recorded in Exodus 34) he similarly but slightly differently described himself as:

> The Lord, the Lord, a merciful and gracious God, slow to anger and rich in kindness and fidelity, continuing his kindness for a thousand generations, and forgiving wickedness and crime and sin; yet not declaring the guilty guiltless, but punishing children and grandchildren to the third and fourth generation for their fathers' wickedness!
> (Exodus 34:6-7)

It is not so well remembered, however, that the later Reform Prophet Jeremiah and the exile Prophet Ezekiel both thoroughly rejected this "jealous God" theology:

> In those days they shall no longer say, "The fathers ate unripe grapes, and the children's teeth are set on edge," but through his own fault only shall anyone die: the teeth of him who eats the unripe grapes shall be set on edge.
> (Jeremiah 31:29-30)

> Thus the word of the Lord came to me: Son of man, what is the meaning of this proverb that you recite in the land of Israel: "Fathers have eaten green grapes, thus their children's teeth are on edge"? As I live, says the Lord GOD: I swear that there shall no longer be anyone among you who will repeat this proverb in Israel. For all lives are mine; the life of the father is like the life of the son, both are mine; only the one who sins shall die. ... The son shall not be charged with the guilt of his father, nor shall the father be charged with the guilt of his son.
> (Ezekiel 18:1-20)

While it's true that Jeremiah 32:18a *does* include the jealous God motif, it is only as the first of five traditional acclamations of the "mightiness of God":

1) You continue your kindness through a thousand generations; and *you repay the fathers' guilt, even into the lap of their sons* who follow them. (Jer 32:18a)

2) O God, great and mighty, whose name is Lord of hosts, great in counsel, mighty in deed, whose eyes are open to all the ways of men, *giving to each according to his ways, according to the fruit of his deeds*: (Jer 32:18b-19)

3) you have wrought signs and wonders in the land of Egypt and to this day, both in Israel and among all other men, until now you have gained renown. (Jer 32:20)

4) With strong hand and outstretched arm you brought your people Israel out of the land of Egypt amid signs and wonders and great terror. (Jer 32:21)

5) This land you gave them, as you had promised their fathers under oath, a land flowing with milk and honey. (Jer 32:22)

The fact that the second acclamation, *"giving to each according to his ways, according to the fruit of his deeds,"* contradicts the first acclamation, *"repay the fathers' guilt, even into the lap of their sons,"* lends support to the suggestion that the first is simply a reflexive recitation of a traditional praise phrase.

On Scriptural Inerrancy

Just as the rival Aaronid and Mushite priesthoods had no qualms about denying the truth of their rival's claims in (what would became) Scripture, the Reform Prophets also had no qualms about denying the truth of priestly claims in (what would became) Scripture. The above example of Jeremiah rejecting the claim that God was a jealous (and unjust) God who punished children for the sins of their fathers illustrates well his charge that the "lying pen of the scribes" had changed the law of the Lord into falsehood. The "jealous God" theology portrayed God as an unpredictable petty tyrant, completely at odds with the "just God" portrayed by the Reform Prophets; not only did it diminish God, it empowered the priesthood since a jealous, frightening God needs to be propitiated, and the priests would do just that ... for a tithe.

Similarly, the priestly claims (which became Scripture) that the feasts, sacrifices, offerings, and songs, the New Moons, Sabbaths, rituals and convocations were important to and required by God were rejected by Reform Prophets:

"But if you would offer me holocausts, then let justice surge like water, and goodness like an unfailing stream."
(Amos 5:23-24)

"For it is love that I desire, not sacrifice, and knowledge of God rather than holocausts."
(Hosea 6:6)

"Is not this the kind of fasting I have chosen: to loose the chains of injustice and untie the cords of the yoke, to set the oppressed free and break every yoke?"
(Isaiah 58:6)

Whenever there is a teaching in Scripture that diminishes God and conveys power to a favored group, we should suspect it as being a "teaching of Men" rather than a teaching of God ... a "weed among the wheat." The Reform Prophets, the Spokesmen for God, detected these weeds and spoke against them unwaveringly. ... It is as if these Spokesmen had a sieve – a *"Sieve of the Spokesmen,"* if you will – for winnowing out false teachings. If such a sieve had existed, it might read like this:

> *If a teaching gives glory to God,*
> *... showing him to be loving, just, and merciful;*
> *If a teaching shows God to be all-powerful,*
> *... not dependent upon man for anything;*
> *If a teaching humbles man,*
> *... showing him to be needful of God in all things*
> *... and the servant of his fellow men;*
> *The teaching is true.*

❧

> *If a teaching takes glory from God,*
> *... making him appear unloving, unjust, or unmerciful;*
> *If a teaching limits God's power to act*
> *... until man has accomplished something;*
> *If a teaching puffs man up,*
> *... setting man equal to God*
> *... or giving him or his group power over others;*
> *The teaching is false.*

This is the criterion we, too, should use in weighing Scriptural teachings. … It helps to counteract our tribal tendency to make pronouncements in God's name that subtly or blatantly favor our own tribes and denominations, and thus justify the world's skepticism about our claims to goodness.

On a Transcendent Rather Than Tribal God

Despite Israel and Judah's constant warring with other tribes, they had an awareness of an obligation to be fair and kind to individuals from other tribes, "aliens," when they were living in their midst. This awareness is evidenced throughout the biblical source documents. The early E document instructs:

> "You shall not molest or oppress an alien, for you were once aliens yourselves in the land of Egypt. You shall not wrong any widow or orphan. If ever you wrong them and they cry out to me, I will surely hear their cry. My wrath will flare up, and I will kill you with the sword"
> (Exodus 22:20-23)

> "You shall not oppress an alien; you well know how it feels to be an alien, since you were once aliens yourselves in the land of Egypt."
> (Exodus 23:9)

The later P document's rewriting of the combined JE document exhorts:

> "When an alien resides with you in your land, do not molest him. You shall treat the alien who resides with you no differently than the natives born among you; have the same love for him as for yourself; for you too were once aliens in the land of Egypt."
> (Leviticus 19:33)

> "When you reap the harvest of your land, you shall not be so thorough that you reap the field to its very edge, nor shall you glean the stray ears of your grain. These things you shall leave for the poor and the alien."
> (Leviticus 23:22)

The D document rebuttal of the P document reiterates the obligation to be kind and caring to the alien:

> "For the Lord, your God, is the God of gods, the Lord of lords, the great God, mighty and awesome, who has no favorites, accepts no bribes; who executes justice for the orphan and the widow, and befriends the alien, feeding and clothing him. So you too must befriend the alien, for you were once aliens yourselves in the land of Egypt."
> (Deuteronomy 10:17-19)

> "When you reap the harvest in your field and overlook a sheaf there, you shall not go back to get it; let it be for the alien, the orphan or the widow, that the Lord, your God, may bless you in all your undertakings. When you knock down the fruit of your olive trees, you shall not go over the branches a second time; let what remains be for the alien, the orphan and the widow. When you pick your grapes, you shall not go over the vineyard a second time; let what remains be for the alien, the orphan, and the widow.
> (Deuteronomy 24:19-21)

And finally, the Redactor who combined all of the sources into their final form added:

> "... any alien residing with you permanently or for a time, who presents a sweet-smelling oblation to the Lord, shall do as you do. There is but one rule for you and for the resident alien, a perpetual rule for all your descendants. Before the Lord you and the alien are alike, with the same law and the same application of it for the alien residing among you as for yourselves."
> (Numbers 15: 14-16)

While Judaism always recognized a God-ordained obligation to be Good to those in need within their tribes – to the widows, the orphans, and the poor – that they extended this obligation to individuals from other tribes living among them was a major step forward in Religion. To be Good toward tribemates is a God-given instinct, but it is not instinctive to be Good to non-tribemates living among you; achieving that required overriding the instinct to harm and kill non-tribemembers.

Despite this step forward, while alien *individuals* among them (and at their mercy) could be tolerated, alien *tribes* could not: God was still worshipped as a tribal god favoring Israel, with little suggestion that he was a transcendent God of all the nations, with an intense desire that his people – all his people – be Good and caring of one another. Because of the writings, teachings, and actions of the 8th Century B.C.E. Reform Prophets, however, the latter view acquired an enduring voice.

It is hard to realize just how radical that view was when first introduced, challenging not only the reigning kings and courts, but the very crux of our human tribal nature as well. Accepting that God might care for other tribes as much as ours, and worse, that other tribes may not be as evil as we see them, is not something easily embraced. … Thus, we are still struggling today to acknowledge and overcome the extent of our tribal instincts.

Admittedly, the majority of the Reform Prophets writings stressed how God wanted his people to be *within* their tribes: to care for the widows and orphans, to not trample on the heads of the poor or deny justice to the oppressed, to seek justice, and to love mercy. They called on the kings, princes, priests, and rulers, those who "add house to house, and join field to field," to reform their ways, to stop doing wrong, and to learn to do right.

But they didn't stop there: they hinted that God was the God of all the nations, and that all nations would eventually have a relationship with God equal to Israel's. They hinted this hesitantly, but given the prevailing, overwhelming belief that God was the God of Israel only, and that he would lead Israel in subduing or destroying all the other nations and their gods, it is remarkable that they hinted this at all.

And one Prophet, one time, didn't just hint … one time, Amos spoke bluntly:

"Are you not like Ethiopians to me, O men of Israel, says the Lord? Did I not bring the Israelites from the land of Egypt as I brought the Philistines from Caphtor and the Arameans from Kir?"
Amos 9:7)

Except for this astonishing pronouncement, prophetic awareness that God was the God of all nations – of all Mankind – was expressed only when envisioning the End Times ... the new heavens and the new Earth:

> Although the Lord shall smite Egypt severely, he shall heal them; they shall turn to the Lord and he shall be won over and heal them. On that day there shall be a highway from Egypt to Assyria; the Assyrians shall enter Egypt, and the Egyptians enter Assyria, and Egypt shall serve Assyria. On that day Israel shall be a third party with Egypt and Assyria, a blessing in the midst of the land, when the Lord of hosts blesses it: "Blessed be my people Egypt, and the work of my hands Assyria, and my inheritance, Israel."
> (Isaiah 19:22-25)

> I come to gather nations of every language; they shall come and see my glory. ... and they shall proclaim my glory among the nations ... just as the Israelites bring their offering to the house of the Lord in clean vessels. Some of these I will take as priests and Levites, says the Lord. As the new heavens and the new earth which I will make shall endure before me, says the Lord, so shall your race and your name endure. From one new moon to another, and from one sabbath to another, all mankind shall come to worship before me, says the Lord.
> (Isaiah 66:18-23)

> My name will be great among the nations, from the rising to the setting of the sun. In every place incense and pure offerings will be brought to my name, because my name will be great among the nations," says the LORD Almighty.
> (Malachi 1:11)

It is not easy for tribal Man, ancient or modern, to acknowledge and accept that God cares as much for other tribes as his own, and that God's will is that we should *all* be Good one to another. Nonetheless, that is where the hesitant, first steps of the Reform Prophets lead.

This emphatically, however, does *not* mean that all religious tribes are equally Good: whether tribes are "Good" or "Evil" is measurable by how they treat minorities within, and to what degree they tolerate and cooperate with rivals without. Being loving, caring, understanding, and forgiving overrides imposing rituals, sacraments, and doctrines; these latter should be crutches, not clubs. The Reform Prophets sowed the seeds for this enlightenment, and the question is whether we will prove fertile or barren soil for those seeds.

So, given that our hardwired tribal nature predisposes us to fear and harm other tribes, how are we to overcome these predispositions? ... The answer is, "In the way God created and evolved us to override our animal instincts: through a cultural sheath of firmwired programming" ... as discussed next in *Overriding Wisdom*.

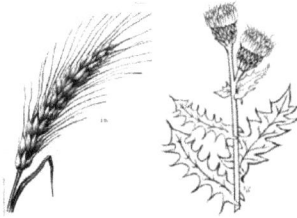

Chapter 6.
Overriding Wisdom

Wisdom teachings have been a civilizing influence throughout human history, counseling us how to rise above our negative instincts and to survive and triumph in our relationships with other individuals and groups in our tribes. In retrospect, it can be realized that firmwired beliefs, often in the guise of wisdom teachings, have always been providing us the means of overriding our hardwired instincts with a sheath of cultural restraints. While our behavior is *predisposed* by our instincts, thanks to our ability to override them with wisdom teachings, laws, and other societal norms, our behavior is not *predestined* ... we *do* have free will.

This can be seen most clearly in our response to the powerful instinct to copulate, to reproduce: despite this instinct's power, there is not now and probably never has been any human society that has given carte blanche to unrestricted sexual licentiousness. In all civilizations having written laws, ancient or modern, the sexual behaviors permitted and forbidden are spelled out in great detail; the details differ from civilization to civilization and society to society, but all limit unbridled sexual indulgence. While the sexually explicit carvings in the temples of Angkor Wat raise the possibility that their civilization may have been an exception to this rule, it's more likely the depicted behavior was the privilege of a ruling or priestly caste, not the whole society. … It could be argued, and I do, that not only is it *normal* for human tribes to place cultural restrictions upon instinctive behaviors, it is *necessary*. We were created/evolved to function in this way … to eternally bridle our "fleshly" animal instincts with societal (tribal) restrictions. It is no burden for us: we naturally and unconsciously form beliefs that foster tribal harmony, and encode the beliefs as law codes and accepted community standards.

Once kings and kingdoms (and their equivalents in other cultures) evolved to replace chieftains and clans, they became the norm for human tribes for millennia; only in the last three centuries of human history have secular dictatorships and democracies evolved as alternatives to kingships. Since Hebrew Wisdom literature emerged within the milieu of kings, courts, priests, and prophets, it employs the language and imagery of that milieu, and teaches how to cope, survive, and even prosper within it.

In English translations of the Bible, "wisdom" appears in two guises: lowercase, as when speaking of "having," "teaching," or "speaking" wisdom …

> Teach me wisdom and knowledge, for in your commands I trust.
> (Psalm. 119:66)

and capitalized, as "Wisdom" …

> Wisdom instructs her children and admonishes those who seek her.
> (Sirach 4:11)

In lowercase "wisdom" is proximately a synonym for "understanding": knowledge is good, but understanding – wisdom – is needed to apply knowledge correctly; in uppercase wisdom becomes personified into "Wisdom," a demigoddess that remonstrates with us and instructs us. Both forms are intermixed throughout the Bible's wisdom literature.

Our human appeal to wisdom is not limited to religious writings but is prominent in secular writings as well. When religious literature personifies wisdom, it is almost always as the feminine persona, Wisdom, calming, soothing, counseling, and redirecting angry, self-destructive male impulses. When secular literature personifies wisdom, however, it is often as the masculine persona, "Reason," appealing to logic rather than to God or gods. Whenever wisdom teachings are directed at relationships *between* tribes (especially nations) rather than *within* tribes, it is typically secular and in the guise of Reason rather than Wisdom; thus the Enlightenment thinkers and America's Founding Fathers frequently appealed to Reason in their writings.

While Reason is referenced in the secular world more often than Wisdom, in the religious world Wisdom predominates: searching Scripture for personified Reason (as opposed to "for this *reason*," or "beyond *reason*," etc.) yields no citations, but searching for personified Wisdom yields many ... all within the seven "Wisdom books" of the Bible.

The Wisdom books (cumbersomely called "Sapiential books" by scholars) are:

- Job
- Song of Songs
- Wisdom (or Wisdom of Solomon)
- Sirach (or Ecclesiasticus)
- Proverbs
- Psalms
- Ecclesiastes

As we have already seen with the Historic books, the Wisdom books were assembled over a long period of time by various authors and editors, and it is not always possible to state unambiguously that a particular wisdom section was written at a particular time, by particular persons, for a particular purpose; this can sometimes be done, but more often not. Happily, this does not matter, for wisdom writings address unchanging human nature and are applicable at all times to all people.

Most Bibles – and all Bible commentaries – have extensive summaries and descriptions of the Wisdom books, so I'll provide only a brief review before considering why the Wisdom books address human behavior *within* tribes, but remain mostly silent about human behavior *between* tribes.

✦✦✦

Job and the Song of Songs

Job and the Song of Songs are very unique books in that they instruct by telling a dramatic story in poetic form and allowing the reader to absorb the underlying wisdom. Job is comparable to a Socratic dialog, with different characters presenting different viewpoints on the perplexing problem of why God allows suffering on Earth. The Song of Songs is a love poem written as a dialog between two lovers, but serving as an analogy of the love between God and his people. Because the wisdom of Job and the Song of Songs is subjective and implicit rather than explicit, I will not incorporate it further.

Wisdom and Sirach

Wisdom and Sirach are "Deuterocanonical" or "Apocryphal" books, meaning that not all Jewish, Catholic, and Protestant ecclesiastical bodies have accepted them as authoritative throughout their history. Ecclesiastical bodies, being tribal, are susceptible to accepting or rejecting books as much on whether their opponents do (or do not) as on perceived merit. ... I will treat them equally with the canonical Wisdom books.

Wisdom is believed to have been written about 100 B.C. by an unknown member of the Jewish community at Alexandria. It is often described as having three sections: the first (Chaps 1-6) is addressed to all the rulers of the earth and counsels them to love justice because Wisdom will not dwell with injustice. It extensively condemns a debased form of Epicureanism apparently prevalent at the time (of the "eat, drink, and be merry, for tomorrow we will die" variety) and extols virtuous living even when experiencing suffering at the hands of the irreligious. The second section (Chaps 7-9) is an oration by a speaker (unnamed, but assumed to be Solomon) who extols Wisdom as a mystic force permeating all Creation and active in every good aspect of life. The third section (Chaps 10-19) recounts highlights of Hebrew history (beginning with Adam, describing but not naming the participants), and extols how Wisdom was active throughout. Beginning in Chapter 11, however, it subtly transitions from praising Wisdom to praising God, perhaps indicating the adaptation of an earlier work.

Sirach (Ecclesiasticus) is believed to have been written in Hebrew by a Jerusalem sage about 200 B.C. and – according to its foreword – translated into Greek by his grandson in Egypt sometime after 132 B.C.. Its alternate name, "Liber Ecclesiasticus," or "Church Book," resulted from its extensive use in the early church. Its moral teachings address all aspects of human life in memorable ways, such as "Be swift to hear, but slow answer," and "Mourn with those who mourn." Chapters 44-50 recall all the Hebrew biblical heroes from Adam to Zerubbabel and extols their deeds, faithfulness, and wisdom. The closing chapter relates how seeking Wisdom has saved the author throughout his life, and encourages the reader, "Come aside to me, you untutored, and take up lodging in the house of instruction."

Proverbs

Scholars often describe Proverbs as a "collection of collections" of Wisdom teachings, and believe they were written over an extended period of time. Tradition attributes all of the Proverbs to King Solomon, but internally only two of the sections (collections) are directly attributed to Solomon; two others are attributed to "The Wise," two others to the kings Agur and Lemuel, and the remainder are unattributed. The Hebrew word translated as "Proverbs" doesn't have the implication of "short, pithy sayings" as does the English word, but encompasses a wide range of dramatic forms from aphorisms to dramatic personifications. While about half of the book *is* made up of short sayings we readily identify as "proverbs," the remainder is made up of longer teaching units and styles.

Psalms

The Hebrew title of the Book of Psalms means "Praises," but its English title comes from the Greek translation, "Psalmoi," meaning "songs sung to a harp." The book's 150 psalms are divided into five sections of unequal lengths, each section ending with a benediction. Some scholars believe these divisions were made by the book's final editor (Ezra?) to mirror the five books of the Torah, but others believe the divisions predate this time. Psalms, like Proverbs, contains numerous sub-collections (Elohistic, Psalms of Ascent, Psalms of the sons of Korah, Psalms of Asaph, etc.) which may originally have been independent. Many of the psalms (116 of the 150) have an introductory comment providing supplementary information, such as the purported author, the conditions under which it was written, or, since the psalms were written to be sung as hymns, musical directions for the leader. In the twentieth century scholars began categorizing the psalms into arbitrary "types" (such as community songs of thanksgiving, individual songs of thanksgiving, community laments, individual laments, royal psalms, wisdom psalms, etc.) but acknowledging that not all the psalms fit neatly into only one category.

Ecclesiastes

The title "Ecclesiastes" is (follow this) a Latin transliteration of the Greek translation of the Hebrew word, "Qoheleth," which has traditionally been interpreted as "Teacher" or "Preacher." It was written as the summation of the wisdom learned over a lifetime by "*David's son, Qoheleth, king in Jerusalem*," and was long assumed to be by King Solomon. Its late period Hebrew and other evidence, however, indicates it was written only about three centuries before Christ, and it is now generally accepted that the attribution was (as is not uncommon in religious writings) to increase its acceptance. ... That was probably "wise," since Ecclesiastes challenged prevailing religious ideas with iconoclastic teachings such as:

> "A thankless task God has appointed for men to be busied about."
> (Eccl 1:13b)

> "For in much wisdom there is much sorrow, and he who stores up knowledge stores up grief."
> (Eccl 1:18)

> "Who knows if the life-breath of the children of men goes upward and the life-breath of beasts goes earthward?"
> (Eccl 3:21)

> "Guard your step when you go to the house of God. Let your approach be obedience, rather than the fools' offering of sacrifice; for they know not how to keep from doing evil."
> (Eccl 4:17)

While Hebrew wisdom literature clearly has many differing voices, those voices – like those of the Prophets – together form a "mighty chorus" with a distinguishing leitmotif: *Wisdom comes from God; fear of the Lord is the beginning of Wisdom.* This insistence, notably absent from secular wisdom, permeates all Hebrew wisdom literature. The misfortune is that when the Wisdom books were written, God – with rare exception – was seen as Yahweh, the tribal God of Israel, rather than as the transcendental God of all the nations. Since allegiance to Yahweh inherently precluded any thought of peaceful coexistence with other tribes and their false gods, there is almost no Hebrew wisdom literature directly addressing living peacefully with other tribes.

Christians are faced with a similar dilemma: given the Christian doctrine that only those who acknowledge Jesus Christ as the Son of God are saved, and the Christian "Great Commission" to *make* disciples of all the nations, how can

Christians justify *not* contending with non-Christian nations rather than coexisting with them? ... Only the new vision and understanding of God emerging from the teachings of Jesus can make this possible, but as we will see in Part 2, weeds springing from our tribal nature continue to mingle with wheat in the New Testament as well.

The width, breadth, and depth of Hebrew Wisdom literature is magnificent; it encompasses almost all aspects of human relationships with each other and the archetypal subtribes within human societies: no attempt to summarize it can possibly do it justice. Rather than being a summary, the following paragraphs selectively illustrate Hebrew wisdom literature providing guidance for living a good and God-fearing life in the midst of frequently godless societies. To impose organization on the material, I have grouped the illustrations into arbitrary categories of human relationships:

- Relationships with God;
- Relationships with Family;
- Relationships with Community/Peers;
- Relationships with Opponents/Enemies;
- Relationships with Rulers/Powerful;
- Relationships with Poor/Needy;
- Relationships with Foolish/Unbelievers.

Following the illustrative wisdom selections we will examine how weeds can arise among the wheat even in Wisdom literature.

Relationships with God

All wisdom comes from the Lord and with him it remains forever.
(Sirach 1:1)

The fear of the Lord is the beginning of knowledge; wisdom and instruction fools despise.
(Proverbs 1:7)

When God, in the beginning, created man, he made him subject to his own free choice. If you choose you can keep the commandments; it is loyalty to do his will. There are set before you fire and water; to whichever you choose, stretch forth your hand. Before man are life and death, whichever he chooses shall be given him.
(Sirach 15:14-17)

Happy those who do not follow the counsel of the wicked, nor go the way of sinners, nor sit in company with scoffers. Rather, the law of the Lord is their joy; God's law they study day and night. They are like a tree planted near streams of water, that yields its fruit in season; Its leaves never wither; whatever they do prospers.
(Psalm 1:1-3)

Trust in the Lord with all your heart, on your own intelligence rely not; In all your ways be mindful of him, and he will make straight your paths. Be not wise in your own eyes, fear the Lord and turn away from evil;
(Proverbs 3:5-7)

As a father has compassion on his children, so the Lord has compassion on the faithful. For he knows how we are formed, remembers that we are dust.
(Psalm 103:13-14)

The last word, when all is heard: Fear God and keep his commandments, for this is man's all; because God will bring to judgment every work, with all its hidden qualities, whether good or bad.
(Eccl 12:13-14)

Relationships with Family

Children, pay heed to a father's right; do so that you may live. For the Lord sets a father in honor over his children; a mother's authority he confirms over her sons. He who honors his father atones for sins; he stores up riches who reveres his mother.
(Sirach 3:1-3)

Hear, my son, your father's instruction, and reject not your mother's teaching; A graceful diadem will they be for your head; a torque for your neck.
(Proverbs 1:8-9)

A wise son makes his father glad, but a foolish son is a grief to his mother.
(Proverbs 10:1)

Train up a child in the way he should go: and when he is old, he will not depart from it.
(Proverbs 22:6)

Happy the husband of a good wife, twice-lengthened are his days; A worthy wife brings joy to her husband, peaceful and full is his life. A good wife is a generous gift bestowed upon him who fears the Lord;
(Sirach 26:1-3)

When one finds a worthy wife, her value is far beyond pearls. Her husband, entrusting his heart to her, has an unfailing prize. She brings him good, and not evil, all the days of her life.
(Proverbs 31:10-12)

A brother is a better defense than a strong city, and a friend is like the bars of a castle.
(Proverbs 18:19)

Relationships with Community/Peers

Be consistent in your thoughts; steadfast be your words. Be swift to hear, but slow to answer. If you have the knowledge, answer your neighbor; if not, put your hand over your mouth.
(Sirach 5:12-14)

Keep away from your enemies; be on your guard with your friends. A faithful friend is a sturdy shelter; he who finds one finds a treasure. A faithful friend is beyond price, no sum can balance his worth.
(Sirach 6:13-15)

Before investigating, find no fault; examine first, then criticize. Before hearing, answer not, and interrupt no one in the middle of his speech. Dispute not about what is not your concern; in the strife of the arrogant take no part.
(Sirach 11:7-9)

He does a kindness who lends to his neighbor, and he fulfills the precepts who holds out a helping hand. Lend to your neighbor in his hour of need, and pay back your neighbor when a loan falls due; Keep your promise, be honest with him, and you will always come by what you need.
(Sirach 29:1-3)

Quarrel not with a man without cause, with one who has done you no harm. Envy not the lawless man and choose none of his ways:
(Proverbs 3:31-32)

A mild answer calms wrath, but a harsh word stirs up anger. The tongue of the wise pours out knowledge, but the mouth of fools spurts forth folly.
(Proverbs 15:1-2)

Again I saw under the sun that the race is not won by the swift, nor the battle by the valiant, nor a livelihood by the wise, nor riches by the shrewd, nor favor by the experts; for a time of calamity comes to all alike.
(Eccl 9:11)

Relationships with Opponents/Enemies

In our prosperity we cannot know our friends; in adversity an enemy will not remain concealed. When a man is successful even his enemy is friendly; in adversity even his friend disappears. Never trust your enemy, for his wickedness is like corrosion in bronze. Even though he acts humbly and peaceably toward you, take care to be on your guard against him.
(Sirach 12:8-11)

Say nothing harmful, small or great; be not a foe instead of a friend; A bad name and disgrace will you acquire.
(Sirach 6:1)

Rejoice not when your enemy falls, and when he stumbles, let not your heart exult, Lest the Lord see it, be displeased with you, and withdraw his wrath from your enemy.
(Proverbs 24:17-18)

If your enemy be hungry, give him food to eat, if he be thirsty, give him to drink; For live coals you will heap on his head, and the Lord will vindicate you.
(Proverbs 25:21-22)

Relationships with Rulers/Powerful

Love justice, you who judge the earth; think of the Lord in goodness, and seek him in integrity of heart; Because he is found by those who test him not, and he manifests himself to those who do not disbelieve him.
(Wisdom 1:1-2)

With all your soul, fear God, revere his priests.
(Sirach 7:29)

Contend not with an influential man, lest you fall into his power.
Quarrel not with a rich man, lest he pay out the price of your
downfall; For gold has dazzled many, and perverts the character
of princes.
(Sirach 8:1-2)

When invited by a man of influence, keep your distance; then he
will urge you all the more. Be not bold with him lest you be
rebuffed, but keep not too far away lest you be forgotten.
(Sirach 13:9-10)

If you are dining with a great man, bring not a greedy gullet to his
table, Nor cry out, "How much food there is here!"
(Sirach 31:12)

When you sit down to dine with a ruler, keep in mind who is
before you; And put a knife to your throat if you have a ravenous
appetite. Do not desire his delicacies; they are deceitful food.
Toil not to gain wealth, cease to be concerned about it.
(Proverbs 23:1-4)

And now, kings, give heed; take warning, rulers on earth. Serve
the Lord with fear; with trembling bow down in homage, Lest God
be angry and you perish from the way in a sudden blaze of
anger.
(Psalms 2:10-11)

Put no trust in princes, in mere mortals powerless to save. When
they breathe their last, they return to the earth; that day all their
planning comes to nothing. Happy those whose help is Jacob's
God, whose hope is in the Lord, their God.
(Psalm 146:3-5)

Relationships with Poor/Needy

When a poor man speaks they make sport of him; he speaks
wisely and no attention is paid him. A rich man speaks and all
are silent, his wisdom they extol to the clouds. A poor man
speaks and they say: "Who is that?" If he slips they cast him
down.
(Sirach 13: 21-22)

To a poor man, however, be generous; keep him not waiting for your alms; Because of the precept, help the needy, and in their want, do not send them away empty-handed.
(Sirach 29:8-9)

He who oppresses the poor blasphemes his Maker, but he who is kind to the needy glorifies him.
(Proverbs 14:31)

He who shuts his ear to the cry of the poor will himself also call and not be heard.
(Proverbs 21:13)

Happy those concerned for the lowly and poor; when misfortune strikes, the Lord delivers them. The Lord keeps and preserves them, makes them happy in the land, and does not betray them to their enemies.
(Psalm 41:2-3)

For he rescues the poor when they cry out, the oppressed who have no one to help. He shows pity to the needy and the poor and saves the lives of the poor.
(Psalm 72:12-13)

For I know the Lord will secure justice for the needy, their rights for the poor. Then the just will give thanks to your name; the upright will dwell in your presence.
(Psalm 140:13-14)

Relationships with Foolish/Unbelievers

A wise man is silent till the right time comes, but a boasting fool ignores the proper time.
(Sirach 20:6)

A proverb when spoken by a fool is unwelcome, for he does not utter it at the proper time.
(Sirach 20:19)

Like the wheel of a cart is the mind of a fool; his thoughts revolve in circles.
(Sirach 33:5)

The way of the fool seems right in his own eyes, but he who listens to advice is wise. The fool immediately shows his anger, but the shrewd man passes over an insult.
(Proverbs 12:15-16)

Speak not for the fool's hearing; he will despise the wisdom of your words.
(Proverbs 23:9)

Fools say in their hearts, "There is no God." Their deeds are loathsome and corrupt; not one does what is right. God looks down from heaven upon the human race, To see if even one is wise, if even one seeks God. All have gone astray; all alike are perverse. Not one does what is right, not even one.
(Psalm 53:2-4)

Guard your step when you go to the house of God. Let your approach be obedience, rather than the fools' offering of sacrifice; for they know not how to keep from doing evil.
(Eccl 4:17)

The heart of the wise is in the house of mourning, but the heart of fools is in the house of mirth. It is better to hearken to the wise man's rebuke than to hearken to the song of fools; For as the crackling of thorns under a pot, so is the fool's laughter.
(Eccl 7:4-6)

... the just, the wise, and their deeds are in the hand of God. Love from hatred man cannot tell; both appear equally vain, in that there is the same lot for all, for the just and the wicked, for the good and the bad, for the clean and the unclean, for him who offers sacrifice and him who does not. As it is for the good man, so it is for the sinner; as it is for him who swears rashly, so it is for him who fears an oath.
(Eccl 9:1-2)

More weighty than wisdom or wealth is a little folly! The wise man's understanding turns him to his right; the fool's understanding turns him to his left. When the fool walks through the street, in his lack of understanding he calls everything foolish.
(Eccl 10:1-3)

❧❦❧

Considering the exquisiteness of Hebrew wisdom teachings, can there possibly be weeds among the wheat even here? ... Unfortunately, yes, and all too easily. Wisdom – applying knowledge properly – depends upon circumstances, so differing assumptions about the existing circumstances will affect the advice given. For example, we say in folk wisdom "Look before you leap," but also, "He who hesitates is lost"; similarly we say, "Nothing ventured, nothing gained," but also, "A bird in the hand's worth two in the bush." All of these sayings are instructive and appropriate in one circumstance, but inappropriate in another. Wisdom is inevitably intertwined with circumstances, and teachings wise in one circumstance can be unwise in another. Thus the same teaching can be "wheat" in one circumstance, but "weed" in another if misapplied. Underlying assumptions, such as ...

- God is a tribal god, not a transcendental god;
- Kings are devoted to doing God's will;
- God intervenes to reward the Good and punish the Evil;
- God *doesn't* intervene to reward the Good and punish the Evil;

... will all affect the "wisdom" of the Wisdom writings. Examples of Wisdom teachings reflecting these underlying assumptions include:

God is a tribal god, not a transcendental god

Come to our aid, O God of the universe, and put all the nations in dread of you! Raise your hand against the heathen, that they may realize your power. As you have used us to show them your holiness, so now use them to show us your glory. ... Rouse your anger, pour out wrath, humble the enemy, scatter the foe. Hasten the day, bring on the time; crush the heads of the hostile rulers. Let raging fire consume the fugitive, and your people's oppressors meet destruction. Gather all the tribes of Jacob, that they may inherit the land as of old.
(Sirach 36:1-10)

But they called upon the Most High God and lifted up their hands to him; He heard the prayer they uttered, and saved them through Isaiah. God struck the camp of the Assyrians and routed them with a plague.
(Sirach 48:20-21)

In the sanctuary God promised: "I will exult, will apportion Shechem; the valley of Succoth I will measure out. Gilead is mine, mine is Manasseh; Ephraim is the helmet for my head, Judah, my own scepter. Moab is my washbowl; upon Edom I cast my sandal. I will triumph over Philistia." Who will bring me to the fortified city? Who will lead me into Edom?
(Psalm 60:8-11)

How long, Lord? Will you be angry forever? Will your rage keep burning like fire? Pour out your wrath on nations that reject you, on kingdoms that do not call on your name, For they have devoured Jacob, laid waste his home.
(Psalm 79:5-7)

All the nations surrounded me; in the Lord's name I crushed them. They surrounded me on every side; in the Lord's name I crushed them. They surrounded me like bees; they blazed like fire among thorns; in the Lord's name I crushed them. I was hard pressed and falling, but the Lord came to my help.
(Psalm 118:10-13)

You, Lord of hosts, are the God of Israel! Awake! Punish all the nations. Have no mercy on these worthless traitors.
(Psalm 59:6)

The assumption that God in the past was a tribal God (and implicitly still is) allows wisdom teachings that portray hatred and genocide of other tribes as not only permissible, but God ordained. We will see in Part 2 how Jesus' teachings treat this assumption.

Kings are devoted to doing God's will

The king's lips are an oracle; no judgment he pronounces is false. ... Kings have a horror of wrongdoing, for by righteousness the throne endures. The king takes delight in honest lips, and the man who speaks what is right he loves.
(Proverbs 16:10-13)

A king seated on the throne of judgment dispels all evil with his glance.
(Proverbs 20:8)

A wise king winnows the wicked, and threshes them under the cartwheel. ... Kindness and piety safeguard the king, and he upholds his throne by justice.
(Proverbs 20:26-28)

My son, fear the Lord and the king; have nothing to do with those who rebel against them;
(Proverbs 24:21)

O mighty king, lover of justice, you alone have established fairness; you have created just rule in Jacob.
(Psalm 99:4)

The assumption that Kings are devoted to doing God's will allows wisdom teachings that present obedience to kings and authorities as *always* being good, even though the Historical books' provide ample evidence that kings and authorities often disobey God's will: to do God's will in those circumstances requires *opposing* kings and authorities.

God intervenes to reward the Good and punish the Evil.

The Most High himself hates sinners, and upon the wicked he takes vengeance.
(Sirach 12:7)

For mercy and anger alike are with him who remits and forgives, though on the wicked alights his wrath. Great as his mercy is his punishment; he judges men, each according to his deeds. A criminal does not escape with his plunder; a just man's hope God does not leave unfulfilled. Whoever does good has his reward, which each receives according to his deeds.
(Sirach 16:11-14)

No evil can harm the man who fears the Lord; through trials, again and again he is safe.
(Sirach 31:1)

The Lord is a stronghold to him who walks honestly, but to evildoers, their downfall. The just man will never be disturbed, but the wicked will not abide in the land.
(Proverbs 10:29-30)

A shield before me is God who saves the honest heart. God is a just judge, who rebukes in anger every day. If sinners do not repent, God sharpens his sword, strings and readies the bow, Prepares his deadly shafts, makes arrows blazing thunderbolts.
(Psalms 7:11-14)

Many are the troubles of the just, but the Lord delivers from them all. God watches over all their bones; not a one shall be broken. Evil will slay the wicked; those who hate the just are condemned. The Lord redeems loyal servants; no one is condemned whose refuge is God.
(Psalm 34:20-23)

Those who do evil will be cut off, but those who wait for the Lord will possess the land. Wait a little, and the wicked will be no more; look for them and they will not be there. But the poor will possess the land, will delight in great prosperity.
(Proverbs 37:9-11)

God *doesn't* intervene to reward the Good and punish the Evil.

Why, Lord, do you stand at a distance and pay no heed to these troubled times? Arrogant scoundrels pursue the poor; they trap them by their cunning schemes. The wicked even boast of their greed; these robbers curse and scorn the Lord. In their insolence the wicked boast: "God doesn't care, doesn't even exist." Yet their affairs always succeed; they ignore your judgment on high; they sneer at all who oppose them. They say in their hearts, "We will never fall; never will we see misfortune." Their mouths are full of oaths, violence, and lies; discord and evil are under their tongues. They wait in ambush near towns; their eyes watch for the helpless. to murder the innocent in secret. They lurk in ambush like lions in a thicket, hide there to trap the poor, snare them and close the net. The helpless are crushed, laid low; they fall into the power of the wicked, Who say in their hearts, "God pays no attention, shows no concern, never bothers to look."
(Psalm 10:1-11)

My God, my God, why have you abandoned me? Why so far from my call for help, from my cries of anguish? My God, I call by day, but you do not answer; by night, but I have no relief. Yet you are enthroned as the Holy One; you are the glory of Israel. In you our ancestors trusted; they trusted and you rescued them. To you they cried out and they escaped; in you they trusted and were not disappointed. But I am a worm, hardly human, scorned by everyone, despised by the people. All who see me mock me; they curl their lips and jeer; they shake their heads at me: "You relied on the Lord – let him deliver you; if he loves you, let him rescue you."
(Psalm 22:2-9)

Lord, avenging God, avenging God, shine forth! Rise up, judge of the earth; give the proud what they deserve. How long, Lord, shall the wicked, how long shall the wicked glory? How long will they mouth haughty speeches, go on boasting, all these evildoers? They crush your people, Lord, torment your very own. They kill the widow and alien; the fatherless they murder. They say, "The Lord does not see; the God of Jacob takes no notice." (Psalm 94:1-7)

This is a vanity which occurs on earth: there are just men treated as though they had done evil and wicked men treated as though they had done justly. (Eccl 8:14)

The assumption that God *does* intervene to reward the Good and punish the Evil on earth will give rise to teachings that conflict with teachings arising from the assumption that God *doesn't* intervene to reward the Good and punish the Evil. ... Just as in the "*a bird in the hand is worth two in the bush*" vs. "*nothing ventured, nothing gained*" dichotomy, both sets of wisdom teachings may be "wise" or not depending upon the existing circumstances. ... Perhaps in a just society the Good *are* rewarded and the Evil punished, but in an unjust society the Good are punished and the Evil rewarded. ... In Part 2 we will consider the teachings of Jesus that address this conundrum.

❧❧ **Part 2** ❧❧

"Weeds" in the New Testament

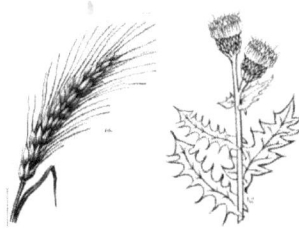

Chapter 7.
The New Testament - An Overview

The writings of the New Testament follow those of the Old Testament in demonstrating both our tribal nature and the presence of Man-inspired weeds among God-inspired wheat. As with the Old Testament, acknowledging weeds among the wheat does not diminish the New Testament's power, but rather enhances it by making understandable many of the issues and paradoxes we argue about rather than practicing love for one another.

The title, "New Testament," reflects the Christian belief that the covenants (testaments) made by God with Israel and recorded in the Hebrew Bible ("Old Testament") have been superseded by a new covenant with *all* who believe in Jesus as the Son of God. The phrase "new covenant" was introduced by the prophet Jeremiah when he wrote,

> "The days are coming, says the Lord, when I will make a new covenant with the house of Israel and the house of Judah." (Jeremiah 31:31)

Jeremiah's phrase is quoted in the book of Hebrews …

> … But he finds fault with them and says: "Behold, the days are coming, says the Lord, when I will conclude a new covenant with the house of Israel and the house of Judah." (Hebrews 8:8)

… and is used in both the Gospel of Luke and Paul's Epistle to the Corinthians to describe the shedding of Jesus' blood as being the instrument of the new covenant …

> And likewise the cup after they had eaten, saying, "This cup is the new covenant in my blood, which will be shed for you."
> (Luke 22:20)

> In the same way also the cup, after supper, saying, "This cup is the new covenant in my blood. Do this, as often as you drink it, in remembrance of me."
> (1 Cor 11:25)

The twenty-seven books that comprise the New Testament were all written within a relatively short period of time – about one hundred-and-twenty years – following the crucifixion and resurrection of Jesus. This tumultuous period saw the Romans' violent suppression of two Jewish revolts, the destruction of Jerusalem and the Jewish Temple, and the dispersion of the surviving Jewish population throughout the Roman empire: some of the books were written before this cataclysm, and some after.

The predominant Jewish groups (tribes) vying for influence both prior to and throughout this period were:

- Priests
- Scribes (Teachers of the Law)
- Pharisees
- Sadducees
- Essenes
- Zealots
- Herodians
- Aramaic speaking Jews
- Greek-speaking Jews
- followers of John the Baptist
- followers of Jesus
- followers of Paul
- followers of Apollos

The New Testament books were all written by followers of Jesus, followers of Paul, or Paul himself, but their writings acknowledge the presence and influence of followers of John the Baptist and followers of Apollos. The Essenes aren't mentioned by name in the New Testament, but their widespread presence is attested to in the writings of Josephus, Philo, and Pliny.

The twenty-seven books began to be collectively referred to as "the New Testament" as early as the third century C.E., and were canonized piecemeal by various regional church councils over the ensuing centuries. Twenty-one of the books are letters addressed to early Christian communities (Epistles), and four are accounts of the life and teachings of Jesus (Gospels). The other two are an account of the spreading of the Christian faith to the Roman empire (Acts) and a veiled prophesy of future times (Revelation.) Since it is universally accepted that Acts is a continuation of the Gospel of Luke by the same author, I will include it with the Gospels, and since Revelation is represented as a letter to "the seven churches in Asia," I will include it with the Epistles.

As observed with the Hebrew Bible's Wisdom literature, "weeds" can arise simply from different writers' having differing viewpoints, emphases, and assumptions. The differences themselves aren't the problem so much as our predisposition to adopt as true only one of competing viewpoints and to then vigorously reject the others. Consequently Christian leaders, both early and modern, have picked and chosen which teachings to emphasize and incorporate into doctrines, and which to ignore. Thus we compulsively argue over "faith versus works," "predestination versus free will," and the many other doctrines dividing Christianity; the result is our splintered Christian kingdom and the scorn of the world.

In the next three chapters we will examine the differing viewpoints, emphases, and assumptions evident *within* the Epistles, *within* the Gospels, and *between* the Epistles and Gospels.

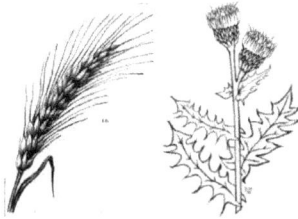

Chapter 8.
Epistles vs. Epistles

Scholars, clergy, and laymen alike have long acknowledged that the twenty-one Epistles (twenty-two, including Revelation) in the New Testament were not intended by their writers to be canonized into theological documents. As collected letters to specific and general communities (with one or two perhaps to an individual), the Epistles could hardly be expected to not have differences in details and emphases, since each community had its own particular circumstances and needs. The letter writers were sometimes concerned with addressing specific community problems and offering encouragement, and at other times with addressing broader theological issues and rejecting heresies. Most of the letters have elements of both concerns in varying degrees.

The many Christian denominations and non-denominations dividing us are the result of different groups selecting different details from the Epistles (and Gospels) to emphasize. Like astrologists linking arbitrarily selected stars to create constellations, we link arbitrarily selected scripture verses to create doctrines. … The Christian schism on whether or not the Bible is "inerrant" also powerfully affects whether different denominations and/or non-denominations view particular verses as wheat or weeds. … It could be said, "The fault, dear Theophilus, lies not in our scripture, but in ourselves."

Because of our familiarity with our own denomination's and/or non-denomination's doctrines and supporting proof texts, it can be disturbing to be made aware that other verses in the Epistles may *not* support them, and may even contradict them. … That is what we will examine now.

꧁꧂

Thanks to the monumental discoveries between 1947 and 1956 of troves of ancient Jewish scrolls hidden in caves near the Dead Sea, more is known now than ever before about first century and earlier Judaism. It is now appreciated that there were many more strands of Jewish thought, religious and sectarian, than had been evidenced by traditional documents. Traditional documents reflect the "winners" in the battle of ideas, and "losing" ideas are often lost or underrepresented. Think, for example, of how few copies have survived of the so-called "lost gospels" of Thomas, Philip, Mary, Peter, Judas, etc. The Dead Sea Scrolls, in contrast, retain and reveal many of the ideas that were contending to become normative Judaism.

We, by nature, do not like having conflicting ideas mingling together. As described in Chapter 1, one of our human tribal traits is the predisposition to adopt as true only one of competing viewpoints, and to then fiercely reject all the others. If our chosen view is challenged by others, we harden it into an absolute dictum that we defend blindly, even to the death.

Being aware of this compulsion, as we consider now the differing details and emphases within the Epistles we should discipline ourselves to remember that our having a preferred viewpoint does *not* render other viewpoints false, just as others having their preferred viewpoints does not render *our* viewpoint false. We must constantly remind ourselves that God wants us to be loving and caring of one another rather than clubbing each other with differing doctrines and interpretations.

꧁꧂

Traditionally the Epistles are divided into two groups: thirteen letters associated with Paul (the Pauline Epistles), and eight (nine, including Revelation) letters associated with others (the General Epistles).

The Pauline Epistles

From the earliest days of the Christian Church doubt has been expressed by various Church leaders/theologians whether all of the

Pauline letters were actually written by Paul. With the advent of critical Bible study and modern methods of minutely examining texts, the evidence for and against Pauline authorship of each of the letters has been assembled and thoroughly debated. Of the thirteen letters attributed to Paul, the scholarly consensus is that seven of them *were* written by Paul, three probably *were not* written by Paul, and that the evidence is inconclusive for the remaining three. As is usual with any scholarly consensus, some scholars disagree vehemently with the majority.

The dates the letters were written are also subject to debate. Those agreed to have been written by Paul can be more narrowly dated, but even then there is some uncertainty. It is not agreed, for example, during which of Paul's many imprisonments his four prison letters (Ephesians, Philippians, Colossians, and Philemon) were written. ... And when it is unsure whether or not Paul was the author, the proposed dates for a letter can vary widely from within Paul's lifetime to significantly later. ... The dates below are representative of majority opinions.

The letters generally agreed to have been written by Paul are:

1st Thessalonians	(ca. 51-52 C.E.)
Philippians	(ca. 55–63 C.E.)
Philemon	(ca. 60–63 C.E.)
1st Corinthians	(ca. 55–57 C.E.)
Galatians	(ca. 48-55 C.E.)
2nd Corinthians	(ca. 56–57 C.E.)
Romans	(ca. 56–58 C.E.)

The inconclusive letters are:

2nd Thessalonians	(ca. 51-54 C.E.)
Colossians	(ca. 60-63 C.E.)
Ephesians	(ca. 62-75 C.E.)

The letters generally agreed to have *not* been written by Paul are:

1st Timothy	(ca. 63-110 C.E.)
2nd Timothy	(ca. 63-110 C.E.)
Titus	(ca. 63-110 C.E.)

While the authorship and dating of the Epistles is a legitimate and necessary concern for scholars, for Christians the overriding concern should be whether the contents of the Epistles are true – whether they reflect teachings of God or teachings of Men – regardless of who wrote them and when.

The General Epistles

As with the Pauline Epistles, from the earliest days of the Christian Church doubt has been expressed by various Church leaders/theologians whether all of the General Epistles were actually written by their stated and/or traditional authors. The proposed dates of their composition consequently can vary widely depending upon whom is assumed to be the author. The dates below, again, are representative of majority opinions.

James	(ca. 48-110 C.E.)
Hebrews	(ca. 63-69 C.E.)
1st Peter	(ca. 63-90 C.E.)
2nd Peter	(ca. 64-130 C.E.)
1st John	(ca. 90-100 C.E.)
2nd John	(ca. 90-100 C.E.)
3rd John	(ca. 90-100 C.E.)
Jude	(ca. 60-80 C.E.)
Revelations	(ca. 68-96 C.E.)

Although the Book of Revelation is unique – an "Apocalypse" – I include it as an "epistle" to "the seven churches in Asia."

Briefly, the scholarly consensus on the authorship of the General Epistles is:

James – Contains the greeting, *"James, a slave of God and of the Lord Jesus Christ, to the twelve tribes in the dispersion."* It does not indicate whether the author is "James the brother of Jesus," or one of Jesus' disciples, "James the son of Zebedee," or "James the son of Alpheus." The majority view is that it was written either by James the brother of Jesus or by a later pseudonymous author. Since it mentions neither God nor Jesus it is sometimes described as New Testament "Wisdom Literature."

Hebrews – Contains no internal claim of authorship, but was once known as "The Epistle of Paul to the Hebrews." It has since become so widely accepted that Paul was *not* the author of Hebrews that it is almost always included in the General Epistles rather than the Pauline Epistles.

1st Peter - Contains the greeting, *"Peter, an apostle of Jesus Christ, to the chosen sojourners of the dispersion."* The early Church widely accepted St. Peter as the author, but critical studies have raised the possibility that it was written by a later, pseudonymous author.

2nd Peter - Contains the greeting, *"Simon Peter, a slave and apostle of Jesus Christ, to those who have received a faith of equal value to ours."* The early Church had some doubts about St. Peter being the author, but not enough to reject it. As with 1st Peter, critical studies have raised the possibility that it was written by a later pseudonymous author.

1st John - Contains no greeting or internal claim of authorship. Because of its great similarity in phrasing and thought with the Gospel of John, however, the majority view is that both were written by the same author ... whether that was John "the Beloved Disciple," John "the Presbyter," or John "of Patmos" is unknown.

2nd John - Contains the greeting, *"The Presbyter (or Elder) to the chosen Lady and to her children."* There is no consensus whether the "chosen Lady" is an individual or a community, or whether "the Presbyter" was also the author of the Gospel of John; there is a slight consensus that he was also the author of 3rd John.

3rd John - Contains the greeting, *"The Presbyter (or Elder) to the beloved Gaius."* There is a slight consensus that 2nd and 3rd John had the same author, but probably one different from the author of the Gospel of John and/or 1st John.

Jude - Contains the greeting, *"Jude, a slave of Jesus Christ and brother of James, to those who are called ..."* (The Greek source actually says "Judas," but this was translated as "Jude," presumably to avoid confusion with Judas Iscariot.) The author of Jude has been traditionally understood by the early Church as being Judas, the brother of Jesus and James.

Revelations - Contains the greeting, *"John, to the seven churches in Asia,"* and the author describes himself as being in exile on the island of Patmos in the Aegean Sea. The author traditionally was assumed to be John the Apostle, but differences in grammar, style, and theological details between the Gospel of John and Revelation suggest a separate author, usually referred to as John "of Patmos."

✦✦✦

Again, regardless of who wrote the Epistles or when, the overwhelming concern for Christians should be whether the teachings in the Epistles are *true*. Teachings that empower Man or diminish God should be recognized as "weeds," and discounted in favor of teachings that honor God and humble Man. We must remember that our confirmation bias – our unconscious predisposition to embrace data that supports our existing beliefs and to discard data that doesn't – continually biases us toward doctrines that flatter *Us* at the expense of others, even God. This is evident in our practice of "proof-texting" … of citing selected scriptural passages as proof that a doctrine is true and justified, while ignoring less supportive or contrary passages.

Because we are so familiar with our preferred Christian doctrines and their proof-texts, it's easy to forget that these doctrines evolved over centuries and were much debated. During that time, long before critical Bible study, the Epistles were generally treated as having equal authority: that is, it was not generally weighed whether some Epistles were more likely than others to have actually been written by Paul or an Apostle, and should consequently be accorded more authority. In the following discussion, to not complicate things needlessly, I too will treat all the Epistles as having equal authority and will abstract from them only sufficient material to illustrate the contention: *Differing doctrines can legitimately be derived from the Epistles; we consequently should cease our denominational (tribal) efforts to impose our preferred doctrines on one another*. We will look at the Epistles' teachings used as proof-texts for doctrines on:

- The Nature of Jesus
- Baptism
- The Requirements for Salvation
- Predestination
- The End Times
- The Last Supper

The Nature of Jesus

If the natures of God, Jesus, and the Holy Spirit were clearly described in Scripture there would have been no need for the centuries of Church councils and resulting Creeds attempting to resolve ambiguities. The Councils and Creeds are witnesses to the many, diverse interpretations given to the relatively scant and autonomous Scripture verses addressing the issues.

Here is what the Epistles tell us about the nature of Jesus:

... though he was in the form of God, did not regard equality with God something to be grasped. Rather, he emptied himself, taking the form of a slave, coming in human likeness; and found human in appearance, he humbled himself, becoming obedient to death, even death on a cross. Because of this, God greatly exalted him and bestowed on him the name that is above every name ...
(Philippians 2:6-9)

... the gospel about his Son, descended from David according to the flesh, but established as Son of God in power according to the spirit of holiness through resurrection from the dead, Jesus Christ our Lord.
(Romans 1:3-4)

He is the image of the invisible God, the firstborn of all creation. For in him were created all things in heaven and on earth, the visible and the invisible, whether thrones or dominions or principalities or powers; all things were created through him and for him. He is the head of the body, the church. He is the beginning, the firstborn from the dead, that in all things he himself might be preeminent. For in him all the fullness was pleased to dwell, and through him to reconcile all things for him, making peace by the blood of his cross (through him), whether those on earth or those in heaven.
(Colossians 1:15-20)

... in these last days, he spoke to us through a son, whom he made heir of all things and through whom he created the universe, who is the

refulgence of his glory, the very imprint of his being, and who sustains all things by his mighty word.
(Hebrews 1:2-3)

For there is one God. There is also one mediator between God and the human race, Christ Jesus, himself human, who gave himself as ransom for all
(1 Timothy 2:5-6)

Summarizing …

- Philippians tells us Jesus was "in the form of God," yet "human in appearance," and that because he humbled himself and was obedient, even to death on the cross, God "exalted him."

- Romans tell us that he descended from David "according to the flesh," but was "established as Son of God in power" "through resurrection from the dead."

- Colossians tells us that he "is the image of the invisible God," that "in him were created all things in heaven and on earth," that "he is the head of the body, the church," and that "he is the beginning, the firstborn from the dead."

- Hebrews tells us God "spoke to us through a son, whom he made heir of all things, and through whom he created the universe," and that he is "the very imprint of his being."

- First Timothy tells us "There is also one mediator between God and the human race, Christ Jesus, himself human, who gave himself as ransom for all."

These portrayals of Jesus as both human and yet the eternal Son of God are similar but not identical, and they leave unanswered details we would like to know: was Jesus aware of his divine mission from conception, or did he became aware of his role gradually through the Holy Spirit and study of Scripture?

How to resolve the differences and fill in missing details were the questions that faced the early Church Councils in their efforts to derive definitive doctrines … doctrines that also had to incorporate additional viewpoints from the Gospels.

Baptism

Here is what the Epistles tell us about Baptism:

... Was Paul crucified for you? Or were you baptized in the name of Paul? I give thanks (to God) that I baptized none of you except Crispus and Gaius, so that no one can say you were baptized in my name. (I baptized the household of Stephanas also; beyond that I do not know whether I baptized anyone else.) For Christ did not send me to baptize but to preach the gospel, and not with the wisdom of human eloquence, so that the cross of Christ might not be emptied of its meaning.
(1 Corinthians 1:13-17)

For in one Spirit we were all baptized into one body, whether Jews or Greeks, slaves or free persons, and we were all given to drink of one Spirit. ...
(1 Corinthians 12:13)

Or are you unaware that we who were baptized into Christ Jesus were baptized into his death? We were indeed buried with him through baptism into death, so that, just as Christ was raised from the dead by the glory of the Father, we too might live in newness of life. For if we have grown into union with him through a death like his, we shall also be united with him in the resurrection.
(Romans 6:3-5)

You were buried with him in baptism, in which you were also raised with him through faith in the power of God, who raised him from the dead.
(Colossians 2:12)

This prefigured baptism, which saves you now. It is not a removal of dirt from the body but an appeal to God for a clear conscience, through the resurrection of Jesus Christ, who has gone into heaven and is at the right hand of God, with angels, authorities, and powers subject to him.
(1 Peter 3:21-22)

The letters of Paul stress that it is through Baptism that believers become one with Christ and one another, and participate in Christ's death and resurrection. Because of his strong emphasis on this role of Baptism, it is surprising to read that he did not feel called to baptize anyone, as he did to preach the gospel.

The letter written by (or in the name of) Peter describes Baptism differently: instead of being the means of becoming one with Christ, it is "an appeal to God for a clear conscience."

None of the Epistles address whether there's a baptism of the Spirit distinct from a baptism with water, whether baptism is only for repentance, or whether baptism is required for salvation. To answer these questions the early church Councils had to turn to the Gospels and Acts, as discussed in the next Chapter.

The Requirements for Salvation

Here is what the Epistles tell us about the requirements for salvation:

For God did not destine us for wrath, but to gain salvation through our Lord Jesus Christ, who died for us.
(1 Thessalonians 5:9-10)

For we must all appear before the judgment seat of Christ, so that each one may receive recompense, according to what he did in the body, whether good or evil.
(2 Corinthians 5:10)

... that no one is justified before God by the law is clear, for "the one who is righteous by faith will live."
(Galatians 3:11)

For I am not ashamed of the gospel. It is the power of God for the salvation of everyone who believes: for Jew first, and then Greek. For in it is revealed the righteousness of God from faith to faith; as it is written, "The one who is righteous by faith will live."
(Romans 1:16-17)

For we consider that a person is justified by faith apart from works of the law. ... God is one and will justify the circumcised on the basis of faith and the uncircumcised through faith.
(Romans 3:28-30)

... while we were still sinners Christ died for us. How much more then, since we are now justified by his blood, will we be saved through him from the wrath.
(Romans 5:8-9)

Or are you unaware that we who were baptized into Christ Jesus were baptized into his death? We were indeed buried with him

through baptism into death, so that, just as Christ was raised from the dead by the glory of the Father, we too might live in newness of life.
(Romans 6:3-4)

if you confess with your mouth that Jesus is Lord and believe in your heart that God raised him from the dead, you will be saved. For one believes with the heart and so is justified, and one confesses with the mouth and so is saved.
(Romans 10:9-10)

You were buried with him in baptism, in which you were also raised with him through faith in the power of God, who raised him from the dead.
(Colossians 2:12)

For by grace you have been saved through faith, and this is not from you; it is the gift of God; it is not from works, so no one may boast.
(Ephesians 2:8)

... not because of any righteous deeds we had done but because of his mercy, he saved us through the bath of rebirth and renewal by the holy Spirit, whom he richly poured out on us through Jesus Christ our savior, so that we might be justified by his grace and become heirs in hope of eternal life.
(Titus 3:5-6)

What good is it, my brothers, if someone says he has faith but does not have works? Can that faith save him? If a brother or sister has nothing to wear and has no food for the day, and one of you says to them, "Go in peace, keep warm, and eat well," but you do not give them the necessities of the body, what good is it?
(James 2:14-16)

Blessed be the God and Father of our Lord Jesus Christ, who in his great mercy gave us a new birth to a living hope through the resurrection of Jesus Christ from the dead, to an inheritance that is imperishable, undefiled, and unfading, kept in heaven for you who by the power of God are safeguarded through faith, to a salvation that is ready to be revealed in the final time. ...
(1 Peter 1:3-5)

This prefigured baptism, which saves you now. It is not a removal of dirt from the body but an appeal to God for a clear conscience, through the resurrection of Jesus Christ ...
(1 Peter 3:21)

... the blood of his Son Jesus cleanses us from all sin. If we say, "We are without sin," we deceive ourselves, and the truth is not in us. If we acknowledge our sins, he is faithful and just and will forgive our sins and cleanse us from every wrongdoing.
(1 John 1:7b-9)

But if anyone does sin, we have an Advocate with the Father, Jesus Christ the righteous one. He is expiation for our sins, and not for our sins only but for those of the whole world.
(1 John 2:1-2)

Summarizing ...

- Thessalonians tells us God destined us for salvation through Jesus who died for us.

- 2 Corinthians tells us we must appear before the judgement seat of Christ and be judged by what we did.

- Galatians and Romans tell us the one who is righteous by faith will live.

- Romans and Colossians tell us that we who are baptized into Jesus' death will be raised with him.

- Romans also tells us that Christ died for us, we are justified by his blood, and that if we confess Jesus is Lord and believe God raised him from the dead we will be saved.

- Ephesians tells us that we have been saved through faith, by grace.

- 1 John tells us that if we acknowledge our sins Jesus will forgive our sins and cleanse us from wrongdoing ... and that Jesus is the expiation of sins for the whole world.

- Titus tells us we are saved through the bath of rebirth and renewal by the holy Spirit, through Jesus Christ our savior, so that we might be justified by his grace.

- James asks us, "What good is it, my brothers, if someone says he has faith but does not have works? Can that faith save him?"

- 1 Peter tells us God gave us a new birth ... through the resurrection of Jesus Christ from the dead ... safeguarded through faith, to a salvation that is ready to be revealed in the final time. ... This prefigured baptism ... is not a removal of dirt from the body but an appeal to God for a clear conscience, through the resurrection of Jesus Christ.

• 1 John tells us ... the blood of Jesus cleanses us from all sin. ... If we acknowledge our sins, he is faithful and just and will forgive our sins and cleanse us from every wrongdoing. ... But if anyone does sin, we have an Advocate with the Father, Jesus Christ, who is the expiation of not only our sins, but those of the whole world.

Depending upon which of these teachings resonate with us the most, we can derive doctrines that Jesus died as the expiation of the sins of the whole world, that he died only for the sins of those who believe in him, or that – regardless of his sacrifice – we must still appear before his judgement seat and be judged according to our deeds. ... The problem, once again, is not that the Epistles provide differing viewpoints on what is required for our salvation, but that we selectively emphasize those that suit us, ignore the rest, and argue interminably with those selecting otherwise.

Predestination

Here is what the Epistles tell us about Predestination:

No trial has come to you but what is human. God is faithful and will not let you be tried beyond your strength; but with the trial he will also provide a way out, so that you may be able to bear it.
(1 Corinthians 10:13)

Each must do as already determined, without sadness or compulsion.
(2 Corinthians 9:7)

Scripture, which saw in advance that God would justify the Gentiles by faith, foretold the good news to Abraham, saying, "Through you shall all the nations be blessed.
(Galatians 3:8)

I say, then: live by the Spirit and you will certainly not gratify the desire of the flesh. For the flesh has desires against the Spirit, and the Spirit against the flesh; these are opposed to each other, so that you may not do what you want.
(Galatians 5:16-17)

We know that all things work for good for those who love God, who are called according to his purpose. For those he foreknew he also predestined to be conformed to the image of his Son, so that he might be the firstborn among many brothers. And those he predestined he also called; and those he called he also justified; and those he justified he also glorified.
(Romans 8:28-30)

Blessed be the God and Father of our Lord Jesus Christ, who has blessed us in Christ with every spiritual blessing in the heavens, as he chose us in him, before the foundation of the world, to be holy and without blemish before him. In love he destined us for adoption to himself through Jesus Christ, in accord with the favor of his will, for the praise of the glory of his grace that he granted us in the beloved. … In him we were also chosen, destined in accord with the purpose of the one who accomplishes all things according to the intention of his will, so that we might exist for the praise of his glory, we who first hoped in Christ.
(Ephesians 1:3-6, 11-12)

… and that they may return to their senses out of the devil's snare, where they are entrapped by him, for his will.
(2 Timothy 2:26)

So submit yourselves to God. Resist the devil, and he will flee from you.
(James 4:7)

Know this first of all, that there is no prophecy of scripture that is a matter of personal interpretation, for no prophecy ever came through human will; but rather human beings moved by the holy Spirit spoke under the influence of God.
(2 Peter 1:20-21)

Can it be determined from these verses to what degree we are predestined to be believers in Jesus, or to what degree we must consciously, with free will, decide to follow him? In Scripture, as in our lives, we regularly find evidence of both, but our human nature predisposes us to prefer one, and to then reject the other.

The End Times

Here is what the Epistles tell us about the End Times:

For if we believe that Jesus died and rose, so too will God, through Jesus, bring with him those who have fallen asleep. Indeed, we tell you

this, on the word of the Lord, that we who are alive, who are left until the coming of the Lord, will surely not precede those who have fallen asleep. For the Lord himself, with a word of command, with the voice of an archangel and with the trumpet of God, will come down from heaven, and the dead in Christ will rise first. Then we who are alive, who are left, will be caught up together with them in the clouds to meet the Lord in the air.
(1 Thessalonians 4:14-17)

For just as in Adam all die, so too in Christ shall all be brought to life, but each one in proper order: Christ the first fruits; then, at his coming, those who belong to Christ; then comes the end, when he hands over the kingdom to his God and Father, when he has destroyed every sovereignty and every authority and power.
(1 Corinthians 15:22-23)

Behold, I tell you a mystery. We shall not all fall asleep, but we will all be changed, in an instant, in the blink of an eye, at the last trumpet. For the trumpet will sound, the dead will be raised incorruptible, and we shall be changed.
(1 Corinthians 15:51-52)

But understand this: there will be terrifying times in the last days. People will be self-centered and lovers of money, proud, haughty, abusive, disobedient to their parents, ungrateful, irreligious, callous, implacable, slanderous, licentious, brutal, hating what is good, traitors, reckless, conceited, lovers of pleasure rather than lovers of God, as they make a pretense of religion but deny its power.
(2 Timothy 3:1-5)

Know this first of all, that in the last days scoffers will come (to) scoff, living according to their own desires and saying, "Where is the promise of his coming?
(2 Peter 3:3-4)

But the day of the Lord will come like a thief, and then the heavens will pass away with a mighty roar and the elements will be dissolved by fire, and the earth and everything done on it will be found out. Since everything is to be dissolved in this way, what sort of persons ought (you) to be, conducting yourselves in holiness and devotion, waiting for and hastening the coming of the day of God, because of which the heavens will be dissolved in flames and the elements melted by fire. But according to his promise we await new heavens and a new earth in which righteousness dwells.
(2 Peter 3:10-13)

... remember the words spoken beforehand by the apostles of our Lord Jesus Christ ... "In (the) last time there will be scoffers who will live according to their own godless desires." These are the ones who cause divisions; they live on the natural plane, devoid of the Spirit.
(Jude 1:18-19)

Once again, the Epistles present us with similar yet differing pictures of the End Times and we are left to choose – and argue over – the one(s) to be preferred.

The Last Supper

Here is all the Epistles tell us about the Last Supper:

The cup of blessing that we bless, is it not a participation in the blood of Christ? The bread that we break, is it not a participation in the body of Christ? Because the loaf of bread is one, we, though many, are one body, for we all partake of the one loaf.
(1 Corinthians 10:16-17)

For I received from the Lord what I also handed on to you, that the Lord Jesus, on the night he was handed over, took bread, and, after he had given thanks, broke it and said, "This is my body that is for you. Do this in remembrance of me." In the same way also the cup, after supper, saying, "This cup is the new covenant in my blood. Do this, as often as you drink it, in remembrance of me." For as often as you eat this bread and drink the cup, you proclaim the death of the Lord until he comes. Therefore whoever eats the bread or drinks the cup of the Lord unworthily will have to answer for the body and blood of the Lord.
(1 Corinthians 11:23-27)

All other New Testament verses describing the Last Supper are in the Gospels of Mark, Matthew, and Luke, which repeat Paul's First Corinthians 11 description almost word for word; only Luke, however, records Jesus as saying, "Do this in memory of me," corresponding to Paul's, "Do this in remembrance of me."

Did Jesus mean "this is my body" and "this is my blood" symbolically, and only want future "Last Suppers" to be memorials to his sacrifice, or did he mean the words literally and was proclaiming that future "Last Suppers" would be reenactments of his sacrifice? ... The Epistles (and Gospels) can be interpreted both ways, and Christianity has been split for centuries over this issue alone.

As we reviewed these proof texts from the Epistles, we probably found ourselves more appreciative and approving of the verses supporting our personal beliefs than those that did not: we cannot help this, it is thoroughly wired into our being. Also wired in, however, is the means of overcoming our innate biases with reason, wisdom, and common sense. Will we? ... Or will we continue to allow our tribal preferences to divide us and negate our witness to the world? ... "The fault, dear Theophilus, lies not in our scripture, but in ourselves."

Our doctrines, of course, are derived not only from proof-texts in the Epistles but also from the Gospels. In the next chapter we'll examine whether proof-texts from the Gospels also contain differences in viewpoints and details that can be deemed "weeds" by non-believers, and in the following chapter we'll consider whether differences in viewpoints between the Epistles and Gospels may also be a source of "weeds."

Chapter 9.
Gospels vs. Gospels

For Christians, the four Gospels are the heart and soul of not only the New Testament but the entire Bible: much more than just a description of Jesus' life, death, and resurrection, they proclaim his teachings, his words of instruction on how Mankind must live to be in obedience to God's will and attain eternal life.

Over the centuries these documents and teachings have been revered, studied, debated … and attacked. Believers study the Gospels to become more Christ-like and better serve God and their fellowman, but others read them to search out ways to discredit them and Christianity. As we should expect by now, this can be done easily since the Gospels, like much of the rest of Scripture, have multiple sources with sometimes differing viewpoints and details.

Great effort has been expended over nearly two millennia to "harmonize" the Gospels – to reconcile, minimize, or smooth over differences – but the differences exist and should not be ignored or glossed over. Many arise simply from differing descriptions of factual or historical events, such as details of the Birth and Resurrection narratives; while these influence our superficial religious trappings of rituals and doctrines, they are of little consequence to the deep, enduring message of Christianity. Others, however, show Jesus' teachings at one time or setting apparently conflicting with his teachings at another time or setting; these *are* of consequence to discerning the deep, enduring message of Christianity, and these conflicts need to be thoroughly examined and understood.

In this chapter we will review what is known and conjectured about the four Gospels' origins, similarities, and differences, and examine some of the verses used as proof-texts for Christian doctrines. As with the Epistles, it should become evident that the problems are not in the Gospels themselves but in our zeal to impose preferred passages and interpretations – and subsequent doctrines and dogmas – on one another.

The Synoptic Gospels and the Gospel of John

Even a casual examination of the Gospels discloses that Mark, Matthew, and Luke record the events of Jesus' life in the same sequence and with sometimes identical wording. Because they present Jesus' ministry so similarly they are called "synoptic" gospels – gospels having the same viewpoint – and it is possible to create Gospel "parallels" displaying them side-by-side to compare corresponding passages. Attempting to add the Gospel of John to these "parallels" is difficult because John differs significantly in events, sequence of events, and wording. Where the Synoptic Gospels describe Jesus' ministry as taking place over one year and describe Jesus as speaking in down-to-earth sayings, John's Gospel describes Jesus' ministry as taking place over three years and describes Jesus as speaking in lofty, often mystical ways. John omits much material found in the Synoptics – notably Jesus' parables and all but one of his miracles – and adds other material unique to John – notably Jesus' early Galilean ministry.

For two millennia much scholarly effort has been expended to understand why the Synoptic Gospels, while similar, have distinctive differences. The consensus is that multiple written and/or oral sources contributed to these Gospels, causing similarities to arise when the same sources were incorporated, and differences to arise when different sources were used. How many independent sources existed and which source(s) came earliest is still debated, but a "four-source hypothesis" is widely accepted.

In the four-source hypothesis the Gospel of Mark was written first and used as the framework for both Matthew and Luke; this explains their common order of events and sometimes identical wording. Since Matthew and Luke also have sets of identical passages that are *not* from Mark, it is hypothesized that these came from a "lost" source (written or oral) of the sayings of Jesus. This source became referred to as "Quelle" (German for "source") or "Q." Besides these two major sources, Matthew and Luke also contain material unique to themselves which is hypothesized to have come from two other lost sources, "M" and "L," probably oral but maybe written.

The Synoptic Gospel Four-Source Hypothesis

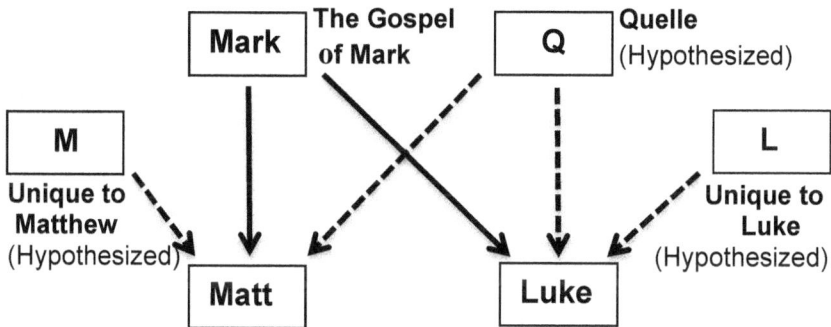

Since scholars also work with other "sayings Gospels" – most notably the Gospel of Thomas – it is now conventional to refer to Q as "the Sayings Gospel Q."

In order to learn more about the Sayings Gospel Q, a team of more than forty scholars led by Dr. James M. Robinson, a prominent New Testament scholar, devoted years to reconstructing Q from all the available early Greek texts of Matthew and Luke. They attempted to determine what the original Q texts must have looked like based (in part) upon whether they were identical in both Matthew and Luke, whether they had been modified to fit Matthew's or Luke's viewpoint, and how the texts changed over time. The results of the studies were published in a *Critical Edition* (for scholars and dedicated laymen) and in a general audience edition, "*The Gospel of Jesus*"; both contain a reconstruction of the Sayings Gospel Q document.

In contrast to Matthew and Luke, the Gospel of John not only doesn't follow the Marcan framework, most of its content is not found in the Synoptics – some scholars claim as much as ninety-percent. It challenges scholars and believers alike with many contrasts: because of its spiritual grace and flowing poetic language it is called "the spiritual Gospel" and "the beloved Gospel," but it is also acknowledged to be the most anti-Semitic Gospel, blanketly ascribing to "the Jews" all the offences the other Gospels ascribe specifically to religious leaders … the Priests, Scribes, and Pharisees.

While the Gospel of John was long thought to be a theological document – i.e., presenting a developed theological narrative rather than historical fact – recent decades of scholarship suggest that John's chronology and description of Jesus' ministry, trial, and crucifixion may be more accurate than the Synoptics, and that they display a significant knowledge of Jerusalem landmarks and Jewish religious practices.

Dating the Gospels

As with the Epistles, the dates the Gospels were written is subject to much scholarly debate. It would be gratifying to have authoritative dates for the Gospels and Epistles, and to be able to see to what degree they overlapped and perhaps influenced each other, but this cannot be done due to the wide range of proposed dates and the lack of proof. For example, while the majority of scholars agree Mark was written first and most date it to around 70 C.E., some scholars date it as early as the 50's and some as late as 80.

One of the ongoing points of contention is why the cataclysmic 70 C.E. destruction of Jerusalem and the Jewish Temple is not explicitly mentioned in the Gospels, particularly since the Synoptic Gospels record Jesus as prophesying of the Temple buildings "*there will not be left here one stone upon another, that will not be thrown down.*" Some scholars argue that this "prophecy" indicates the destruction had already occurred, so the Synoptics had to have been written after 70 C.E.; other scholars argue that if the Synoptics *had* been written after the destruction they almost certainly would have explicitly acknowledged the fulfillment of Jesus' prophecy, so they had to have been written before 70 C.E.. ... Showing once again that whenever there is inconclusive evidence, we make up interpretations that validate our preferred narrative and try to impose our interpretations on others.

Dates currently representative of majority opinions are:

Mark	(ca. 64-70 C.E.)
Matthew	(ca. 70-100 C.E.)
Luke	(ca. 80-100 C.E.)
John	(ca. 90-100 C.E.)

These ranges of dates are sometimes arbitrarily reduced to: "Mark was written about 70, Matthew and Luke were written in the 80's or 90's, and John was written about 100." Again, scholars disagree, some vehemently.

Gospel Differences

Differences between and within the Gospels can be categorized as "factual" (differences in facts) or "teaching" (differences in teachings). Factual differences may be about the events described, the sequence of events, and how Jesus is portrayed; "teaching" differences are differences in what Jesus is portrayed as teaching. Understanding how and why the factual differences came about is important and interesting, but doesn't affect the heart of the Gospels; understanding why Jesus' teachings themselves sometimes appear to be in conflict, however, is vital to Christianity.

Factual Differences

For most non-scholar Christian believers, factual differences between the Gospels present no problem: we simply merge the Gospel narratives in our minds and unconsciously (and then consciously) abstract an overview that incorporates all we believe to be true and ignores the rest. (Remember, however, this is not a "Christian believer" phenomenon, but a *human* phenomenon wired into all of us; it even affects scientists deriving theories from disparate data.)

For example, most Christians are aware that the birth narratives presented in Matthew and Luke (from the unique "M" and "L" sources) are incompatible: Matthew portrays Mary and Joseph as residing in a house in Bethlehem when Jesus is born, being visited by Magi, fleeing to Egypt to escape Herod's infanticide, returning only after Herod's death, and moving to Nazareth in Galilee out of fear of the son of Herod who now ruled Judea; Luke portrays Mary and Joseph as living in Nazareth, traveling to Bethlehem as required by a census, placing the newborn Jesus in a manger, being visited by shepherds, and observantly having Jesus circumcised in Jerusalem while returning to Nazareth.

Rather than arguing over which of these competing and incompatible narratives is "true," Christians tacitly accept that they embody differing oral traditions from different early Christian communities, and unconcernedly portray Matthew's Magi and Luke's shepherds worshipping side-by-side in Christmas pageants.

Similarly, it's tacitly accepted that the Gospels themselves developed in culturally different early Christian communities with independently developed oral traditions, and that each were intended for audiences culturally similar to themselves. Based on internal evidence and writings of early Church fathers, most scholars conclude that Mark was written in a predominantly Roman community with a Roman audience in mind, Matthew in a predominantly Jewish community with a Jewish audience in mind, and Luke and John in predominantly Roman-Greek communities with Roman-Greek audiences in mind. Which *particular* early Christian communities were the birthplaces of the Gospels, however, has not been established. While a majority of scholars suggest Rome for Mark, Antioch for Matthew, Ephesus for John, and various cities for Luke, there is no unanimity.

That culturally different Christian communities distributed throughout the Roman empire should develop differing traditions during the decades from 40 C.E. to 100 C.E. is not surprising. During this tumultuous period the understanding of Jesus' mission was changing from "Jewish teacher and prophet" to "Jewish Messiah and Son of God"; the Jewish capitol, temple, and nation were destroyed; and the Jewish people were exiled throughout the Roman empire.

Under these circumstances, factual differences between the Gospels emerging in culturally different communities should be expected. The remarkable thing is that the Gospels nonetheless *uniformly* record Jesus as ... a charismatic teacher and healer ... having a large following with an innermost band of twelve disciples ... speaking against the false religiosity of the Priests, Scribes, and Pharisees ... being tried and ordered executed by a Roman magistrate ... and rising victorious from the grave. This uniformity exists even across the gulf between the Synoptic Gospels' down-to-earth portrayal of Jesus and his teachings and John's lofty, mystical portrayal of them.

The problem is not that the Gospels emerging from this first century cauldron have factual differences, but that non-believers use them to attack Christianity, and that Christians unwittingly aid them by treating the factual differences as important and contending over them.

Teaching Differences

While the factual differences between the Gospels are of interest they are not significant to the heart and soul of the Gospels, which is Jesus' teachings on doing the will of God ... on how we should live and behave with one another. Apparent differences in what Jesus taught are consequently of utmost importance to Christianity and the world, and should be examined and discussed rather than glossed over.

In the remainder of this chapter we will look at the teachings of Jesus that have been used to develop Christian doctrines, and at other teachings of Jesus that have been largely ignored because they don't reinforce those doctrines. Doing so will validate the contention that: *Differing doctrines can legitimately be derived from the Gospels; we consequently should cease our denominational (tribal) efforts to impose our preferred doctrines on one another.*

Typically, but not always, teachings in Mark are short and direct. When Matthew or Luke incorporate them they sometimes modify them to reflect their communities' understanding of the verses, just as their unique sources, M and L, also reflect their communities' understanding and interpretations. A noticeable (but inconsequential) example of modifications within the Synoptic Gospels can be seen in the teachings on being "for or against" Jesus:

Mark records,

> "For whoever is not against us is for us." (Mark 9:40)

Matthew records the opposite,

> "Whoever is not with me is against me, and whoever does not gather with me scatters." (Matt 12:30)

And Luke incorporates both,

> "For whoever is not against you is for you." (Luke 9:50)

> "Whoever is not with me is against me, and whoever does not gather with me scatters." (Luke 11:23)

Teachings in John differ boldly from the Synoptics in both style and content, reflecting both his community's understanding and viewpoint and the evolving understanding of Jesus' mission as "Jewish Messiah and Son of God" rather than "Jewish teacher and prophet."

Let's look now at the writings within the Gospels that are often used as proof-texts for Christian doctrines on:

- Belief in Jesus is Required for Salvation
- Scriptural Inerrancy
- Reward and Punishment on Earth
- End Times
- Baptism
- The Last Supper

The texts are presented generally in the order Mark-Matthew-Luke-John, but when following texts contain a teaching similar to a preceding one, the following texts have been repositioned to group parallel verses together. (When several texts are essentially identical, the first will be quoted and the others simply noted.)

Belief in Jesus is Required for Salvation

The doctrine that belief in Jesus is required for salvation is supported by many Gospel verses:

Whoever wishes to come after me must deny himself, take up his cross, and follow me. For whoever wishes to save his life will lose it, but whoever loses his life for my sake and that of the gospel will save it.
(Mark 8:34-35)

... and whoever does not take up his cross and follow after me is not worthy of me. Whoever finds his life will lose it, and whoever loses his life for my sake will find it.
(Matt 10:38-39)

Then Jesus said to his disciples, "Whoever wishes to come after me must deny himself, take up his cross, and follow me. For whoever wishes to save his life will lose it, but whoever loses his life for my sake will find it."
(Matt 16:24-25)

Whoever does not carry his own cross and come after me cannot be my disciple.
(Luke 14:27)

———————

Whoever is ashamed of me and of my words in this faithless and sinful generation, the Son of Man will be ashamed of when he comes in his Father's glory with the holy angels.
(Mark 8:38)

Everyone who acknowledges me before others I will acknowledge before my heavenly Father. But whoever denies me before others, I will deny before my heavenly Father.
(Matt 10:32-33)

Whoever is ashamed of me and of my words, the Son of Man will be ashamed of when he comes in his glory ...
(Luke 9:26)

I tell you, everyone who acknowledges me before others the Son of Man will acknowledge before the angels of God. But whoever denies me before others will be denied before the angels of God.
(Luke 12:8-9)

Whoever listens to you listens to me. Whoever rejects you rejects me. And whoever rejects me rejects the one who sent me."
(Luke 10:16)

Whoever does not honor the Son does not honor the Father who sent him.
(John 5:23)

Whoever believes in him will not be condemned, but whoever does not believe has already been condemned, because he has not believed in the name of the only Son of God.
(John 3:18)

———

For this is the will of my Father, that everyone who sees the Son and believes in him may have eternal life, and I shall raise him (on) the last day.
(John 6:40)

I am the resurrection and the life; whoever believes in me, even if he dies, will live, and everyone who lives and believes in me will never die."
(John 11:25-26)

We are very familiar with these verses supporting the doctrine that only those who believe in Jesus will be saved, but we are less aware of verses that suggest otherwise:

*I tell you the truth, **all the sins and blasphemies of men will be forgiven them**. But whoever blasphemes against the Holy Spirit will never be forgiven; he is guilty of an eternal sin.*
(Mark 3:28-29)

> *And so I tell you, every sin and blasphemy will be forgiven men, but the blasphemy against the Spirit will not be forgiven. **Anyone who speaks a word against the Son of Man will be forgiven, but anyone who speaks against the Holy Spirit will not be forgiven**, either in this age or in the age to come.*
> (Matt 12:31-32)

> *... **everyone who speaks a word against the Son of Man will be forgiven, but anyone who blasphemes against the Holy Spirit will not be forgiven**.*
> (Luke 12:10)

> *... **if anyone hears my words and does not observe them, I do not condemn him**, for I did not come to condemn the world but to save the world.*
> (John 12:47)

Where Mark says only that "all sins" will be forgiven except blasphemy against the Holy Spirit, both Matthew and Luke explicitly add that Jesus taught that blasphemy against the Son of Man *will* be forgiven. ... And in Jesus' parable of the Sheep and the Goats, it can be argued that those saved weren't saved because they professed a belief in the Lord (they did not) but because they cared for their fellowman:

> *Then the righteous will answer him and say, 'Lord, when did we see you hungry and feed you, or thirsty and give you drink? When did we see you a stranger and welcome you, or naked and clothe you? When did we see you ill or in prison, and visit you?' And the king will say to them in reply, 'Amen, I say to you, whatever you did for one of these least brothers of mine, you did for me.'*
> (Matthew 25:37-40)

Thus, based on the teachings of Jesus as recorded in the Gospels, it is possible to justify doctrines claiming that belief in Jesus *is* required for salvation, but also doctrines claiming that it *is not*. Because of our tribal nature, we endorse whichever doctrine we – and our denominational tribes – prefer, and try to impose it upon others.

Scriptural Inerrancy

The Gospels depict many confrontations between Jesus and the Priests, Scribes, and Pharisees over what acts are allowed on the Sabbath. Jesus pointed to scripture showing that David and his men violated the Sabbath Law without condemnation, to scripture that specifically overruled general applications of the Law, and to scripture that invoked higher principles ("do good, not evil") to override the letter of the Law when it would be harmful.

> *... At this the Pharisees said to him, "Look, why are they doing what is unlawful on the sabbath? "He said to them, "Have you never read what David did when he was in need and he and his companions were hungry? How he went into the house of God when Abiathar was high priest and ate the bread of offering that only the priests could lawfully eat, and shared it with his companions?" Then he said to them, "The sabbath was made for man, not man for the sabbath. That is why the Son of Man is lord even of the sabbath."*
> (Mark 2:24-28; also Matt 12:2-8 and Luke 6:2-5)

> *... he entered the synagogue. There was a man there who had a withered hand. They watched him closely to see if he would cure him on the sabbath so that they might accuse him. He said to the man with the withered hand, "Come up here before us." Then he said to them, "Is it lawful to do good on the sabbath rather than to do evil, to save life rather than to destroy it?" ... he said to the man, "Stretch out your hand." He stretched it out and his hand was restored.*
> (Mark 3:1-5; also Matt 12:9-13 and Luke 6:6-11)

> *Jesus answered and said to them, "I performed one work and all of you are amazed because of it. Moses gave you circumcision – not that it came from Moses but rather from the patriarchs – and you circumcise a man on the sabbath. If a man can receive circumcision on a sabbath so that the law of Moses may not be broken, are you angry with me because I made a whole person well on a sabbath? Stop judging by appearances, but judge justly."*
> (John 7:21-24)

———————

> *He said to them in reply, "What did Moses command you?" They replied, "Moses permitted him to write a bill of divorce and dismiss her." But Jesus told them, "Because of the hardness of your hearts he wrote you this commandment. But from the beginning of creation, 'God made them male and female. For this reason a man shall leave his father and mother (and be joined to*

his wife), and the two shall become one flesh.' So they are no longer two but one flesh. Therefore what God has joined together, no human being must separate."
(Mark 10:3-9; also Matt 5:31-32 and Matt 19:7-9)

Everyone who divorces his wife and marries another commits adultery, and the one who marries a woman divorced from her husband commits adultery.
(Luke 16:18)

The most striking of these citations is probably Mark 10:3-9 where Jesus could have said, "Moses gave the law about divorce because that was what God commanded," but instead said that he (Moses, not God!) allowed divorce because of the hardness of Men's hearts, and that this was *not* what God intended from the beginning. ... Based on this and the other citations, it is difficult to not conclude that Jesus, like the Reform Prophets, did *not* believe that existing scripture inerrantly reflected the will of God. The "hardness of Men's hearts" – our hearts – allows the adulteration of God's Word with teachings of Men.

Reward and Punishment on Earth

This is a continuation of the debate begun in the Hebrew Bible/Old Testament wisdom literature over whether God does or does not intervene to reward Good and punish Evil. You should recall that a majority of Wisdom literature claims God *does* intervene to reward Good and punish Evil, but that a persistent minority claims God *does not.* My suggestion was that when wisdom teachings conflict with one another it is due to differing underlying assumptions: in a society assumed to be *just* Good is rewarded and Evil punished, but in a society assumed to be *unjust* Good is punished and Evil rewarded.

In Jesus' teachings in the Gospels, however, the differing assumptions aren't the *writers'* assumptions about the nature of their societies, but the *readers' (our)* assumptions over whether Jesus is speaking of material rewards or spiritual rewards. Assuming he is speaking of material rewards enables "health and wealth" ministries promising earthly success as a result of following Jesus. There are plentiful verses to justify this interpretation:

> *The measure with which you measure will be measured out to you, and still more will be given to you. To the one who has, more will be given; from the one who has not, even what he has will be taken away."*
> (Mark 4:24-25)

> *For to everyone who has, more will be given and he will grow rich; but from the one who has not, even what he has will be taken away.*
> (Matt 25:29)

> *Give and gifts will be given to you; a good measure, packed together, shaken down, and overflowing, will be poured into your lap. For the measure with which you measure will in return be measured out to you.*
> (Luke 6:38)

————

> *Therefore I tell you, all that you ask for in prayer, believe that you will receive it and it shall be yours.*
> (Mark 11:24)

> *Whatever you ask for in prayer with faith, you will receive."*
> (Matt 21:22)

> *"Ask and it will be given to you; seek and you will find; knock and the door will be opened to you. For everyone who asks, receives; and the one who seeks, finds; and to the one who knocks, the door will be opened.*
> (Matt 7:7-8)

> *"And I tell you, ask and you will receive; seek and you will find; knock and the door will be opened to you. For everyone who asks, receives; and the one who seeks, finds; and to the one who knocks, the door will be opened. ... If you then, who are wicked, know how to give good gifts to your children, how much more will the Father in heaven give the holy Spirit to those who ask him?"*
> (Luke 11:9-13)

> *If you remain in me and my words remain in you, ask for whatever you want and it will be done for you. By this is my Father glorified, that you bear much fruit and become my disciples.*
> (John 15:7-8)

_____

It was not you who chose me, but I who chose you and appointed you to go and bear fruit that will remain, so that whatever you ask the Father in my name he may give you.
(John 15:16)

And whoever gives only a cup of cold water to one of these little ones to drink because he is a disciple – amen, I say to you, he will surely not lose his reward."
(Matt 10:42)

These teachings, however, are starkly in contrast with other teachings of Jesus calling on his followers to "take up their cross," to disregard material possessions, to expect suffering and persecution as a result of following him, and – most startling – to treat the Evil and the Good alike, just as God does!

He summoned the crowd with his disciples and said to them, "Whoever wishes to come after me must deny himself, take up his cross, and follow me. For whoever wishes to save his life will lose it, but whoever loses his life for my sake and that of the gospel will save it.
(Mark 8:34-35; also Matt 16:24-25 and Luke 9:23-24)

"Whoever loves father or mother more than me is not worthy of me, and whoever loves son or daughter more than me is not worthy of me; and whoever does not take up his cross and follow after me is not worthy of me. Whoever finds his life will lose it, and whoever loses his life for my sake will find it.
(Matt 10:37-39)

Whoever loves his life loses it, and whoever hates his life in this world will preserve it for eternal life.
(John 12:25)

_____

Instead, seek his kingdom, and these other things will be given you besides. ... Sell your belongings and give alms. Provide money bags for yourselves that do not wear out, an inexhaustible treasure in heaven that no thief can reach nor moth destroy. For where your treasure is, there also will your heart be.
(Luke 12:31-34)

... he turned and addressed them, "If any one comes to me without hating his father and mother, wife and children, brothers and sisters, and even his own life, he cannot be my

disciple. .... In the same way, everyone of you who does not renounce all his possessions cannot be my disciple.
(Luke 14:25-33)

But Jesus summoned them and said, "You know that the rulers of the Gentiles lord it over them, and the great ones make their authority over them felt. But it shall not be so among you. Rather, whoever wishes to be great among you shall be your servant; whoever wishes to be first among you shall be your slave. Just so, the Son of Man did not come to be served but to serve and to give his life as a ransom for many."
(Matt 20:25-28)

————————

But rather, love your enemies and do good to them, and lend expecting nothing back; then your reward will be great and you will be children of the Most High, for he himself is kind to the ungrateful and the wicked. Be merciful, just as (also) your Father is merciful
(Luke 6:35-36)

But I say to you, love your enemies, and pray for those who persecute you, that you may be children of your heavenly Father, for he makes his sun rise on the bad and the good, and causes rain to fall on the just and the unjust.
(Matthew 5:44-45)

At that time some people who were present there told him about the Galileans whose blood Pilate had mingled with the blood of their sacrifices. He said to them in reply, "Do you think that because these Galileans suffered in this way they were greater sinners than all other Galileans? By no means! But I tell you, if you do not repent, you will all perish as they did! Or those eighteen people who were killed when the tower at Siloam fell on them—do you think they were more guilty than everyone else who lived in Jerusalem? By no means! But I tell you, if you do not repent, you will all perish as they did!"
(Luke 13:1-5)

The contrast between the verses promising rewards for believing in and following Jesus and those claiming that God does *not* favor or reward the Good over the Evil, ungrateful, and wicked could not be greater, nor more difficult to reconcile. As a consequence, Christianity has proposed many differing interpretations of the collective verses, some claiming the promised rewards are physical rewards on earth, some claiming the rewards are spiritual rewards in heaven … and all generally ignoring the verses claiming God does not reward the Good over the Evil.

End Times

Jesus' teachings on the End Times can be summarized as:

- The End Times are imminent, they will come before the present generation passes away;

- The End Times will occur suddenly, unexpectedly (as with the Flood and Lot);

- The resurrected will not marry, but will be like angels in heaven;

- Signs of the End Times will be:
  - False reports of the Messiah being here;
  - Tribulations (wars, earthquakes, famines, …);
  - Followed by heavenly signs (the sun, moon, and stars will darken or fall, and the Son of Man will appear on clouds of heaven);
  - The Son of Man will separate the good from the bad.

The primary verses supporting these teachings are:

"This is the time of fulfillment. The kingdom of God is at hand. Repent, and believe in the gospel."
(Mark 1:15)

He also said to them, "Amen, I say to you, there are some standing here who will not taste death until they see that the kingdom of God has come in power."
(Mark 9:1; also Matt 16:28)

Amen, I say to you, this generation will not pass away until all these things have taken place. Heaven and earth will pass away, but my words will not pass away. But of that day or hour, no one knows, neither the angels in heaven, nor the Son, but only the Father. Be watchful! Be alert! You do not know when the time will come.
(Mark 13:30-33; also Matt 24:34-36 and Luke 21:32-33)

———

For as it was in the days of Noah, so it will be at the coming of the Son of Man. In (those) days before the flood, they were eating and drinking, marrying and giving in marriage, up to the day that Noah entered the ark. They did not know until the flood came and carried them all away. So will it be (also) at the coming of the Son of Man. Two men will be out in the field; one will be taken, and one will be left. Two women will be grinding at the mill; one will be taken, and one will be left.
(Matt 24:37-40)

As it was in the days of Noah, so it will be in the days of the Son of Man; they were eating and drinking, marrying and giving in marriage up to the day that Noah entered the ark, and the flood came and destroyed them all. Similarly, as it was in the days of Lot: they were eating, drinking, buying, selling, planting, building; on the day when Lot left Sodom, fire and brimstone rained from the sky to destroy them all. So it will be on the day the Son of Man is revealed. On that day, a person who is on the housetop and whose belongings are in the house must not go down to get them, and likewise a person in the field must not return to what was left behind. Remember the wife of Lot. Whoever seeks to preserve his life will lose it, but whoever loses it will save it. I tell you, on that night there will be two people in one bed; one will be taken, the other left. And there will be two women grinding meal together; one will be taken, the other left."
(Luke 17:26-36)

————

Jesus said to them, "Are you not misled because you do not know the scriptures or the power of God? When they rise from the dead, they neither marry nor are given in marriage, but they are like the angels in heaven.
(Mark 12:24-25; also Matt 22:29-30)

Jesus said to them, "The children of this age marry and remarry; but those who are deemed worthy to attain to the coming age and to the resurrection of the dead neither marry nor are given in marriage. They can no longer die, for they are like angels; and they are the children of God because they are the ones who will rise.
(Luke 20:34-36)

Amen, amen, I say to you, the hour is coming and is now here when the dead will hear the voice of the Son of God, and those who hear will live. .... Do not be amazed at this, because the

hour is coming in which all who are in the tombs will hear his voice and will come out, those who have done good deeds to the resurrection of life, but those who have done wicked deeds to the resurrection of condemnation.
(John 5:25-28)

Many will come in my name saying, 'I am he,' and they will deceive many. When you hear of wars and reports of wars do not be alarmed; such things must happen, but it will not yet be the end. Nation will rise against nation and kingdom against kingdom. There will be earthquakes from place to place and there will be famines. These are the beginnings of the labor pains. ... But the gospel must first be preached to all nations ... Brother will hand over brother to death, and the father his child; children will rise up against parents and have them put to death. ... When you see the desolating abomination standing where he should not (let the reader understand), then those in Judea must flee to the mountains.
(Mark 13:6-14; also Matt 24:5-16 and Luke 21:8-11)

But in those days after that tribulation the sun will be darkened, and the moon will not give its light, and the stars will be falling from the sky, and the powers in the heavens will be shaken. And then they will see 'the Son of Man coming in the clouds' with great power and glory, and then he will send out the angels and gather (his) elect from the four winds, from the end of the earth to the end of the sky.
(Mark 13:24-27; also Matt 24:29-31)

When the Son of Man comes in his glory, and all the angels with him, he will sit upon his glorious throne, and all the nations will be assembled before him. And he will separate them one from another, as a shepherd separates the sheep from the goats.
(Matt 25:31-32)

In the teachings on the End Times being imminent Jesus says plainly that even though he does not know the exact time, some of those hearing his words "will not taste death" or "will not pass away" until "the kingdom of God has come" ... until "they see the Son of Man coming in his kingdom." Since the "kingdom of God" did not come in the way his followers expected during the decades the Gospels were being written and since, it required his followers, the early church Fathers, and eventually us to search for deeper understandings of Jesus' teachings on the kingdom/reign of God, and how it can be both "here and now" and yet to come. Those opposing Christianity, however, treat the verses as "weeds," as evidence that the Christian message itself is flawed and unreliable.

The teachings on the signs preceding the End Times and the suddenness with which the End Times will come do not pose any doctrinal issues (except for those who compulsively make doctrinal issues out of every word of Scripture) but the teachings on the nature of post-resurrection bodies do. They raise consideration of not only the nature of post-resurrection bodies, but of the existence and nature of resurrection itself.

The New Testament, like much of the Hebrew Bible, was created in a milieu of both Hebrew culture and the Greco-Roman cultures surrounding it. Thus it is not surprising that the Gospels contain differing but interwoven strands of both Judeo and Greco-Roman beliefs on death and resurrection.

In the oldest Hebrew writings the dead – righteous and unrighteous alike – descend into a place of darkness (Sheol in Hebrew, Hades, in Greek) from which they never return: there is no resurrection. In contrast, Greco-Roman writings from Plato ($\approx$400 B.C.E.) onward portray Man as having a mortal body and an immortal soul, and at death the body perishes to dust but the soul ascends – perhaps for reward or punishment as deserved – and rebirth into a new body.

Over time, hints of Greco-Roman thought and of a resurrection of the dead began to appear in Hebrew scripture. The most cited ones are in Ecclesiastes ($\approx$300 B.C.E.)

> *For the lot of man and of beast is one lot; the one dies as well as the other. Both have the same life-breath, and man has no advantage over the beast; but all is vanity. Both go to the same place; both were made from the dust, and to the dust they both return. Who knows if the life-breath of the children of men goes upward and the life-breath of beasts goes earthward?*
> (Eccl 3:19-21)

and Daniel (≈164 B.C.E.).

At that time there shall arise Michael, the great prince, guardian of your people; It shall be a time unsurpassed in distress since nations began until that time. At that time your people shall escape, everyone who is found written in the book. Many of those who sleep in the dust of the earth shall awake; some shall live forever, others shall be an everlasting horror and disgrace. But the wise shall shine brightly like the splendor of the firmament, And those who lead the many to justice shall be like the stars forever.
(Daniel 12:1-3)

By Jesus' time, there was a clear division between those – notably the Pharisees, Jesus, and his followers – who believed there would be a resurrection of the dead, and those – notably the Sadducees – who retained the traditional belief that there would be no resurrection. The Sadducees ridiculed both the Pharisees and Jesus, enquiring what form "resurrected" bodies raised from dust would take, and if the dead had several spouses in their lives, which one would be their spouse following the resurrection? The Synoptic Gospels record Jesus responding that the resurrected bodies would *not* be the earthly bodies that had died, but a transformed body, perhaps like the angels, that no longer married and would no longer die. The Gospel of John, however, portrays the dead as coming out of their tombs, apparently with their same bodies, to be judged for a "resurrection of life" or a "resurrection of condemnation," with no indication of what form the resurrected bodies would then take.

The majority of Christianity today – as evidenced by our funeral sermons and services – believe that we have immortal souls that leave our bodies at death and are immediately (or after Purgatory) united with God and Jesus in Heaven where they dwell for eternity; but we also believe – as evidenced by our various creeds and doctrines – that there will be a resurrection of the body in some form at the End Times. There is no generally accepted doctrine unifying these two beliefs, but this does not bother us anymore than do the conflicting stories on the birth of Jesus. ... That is, not until someone or some group insists on a particular interpretation ... then it bothers us greatly. It seems that *we ourselves* can be weeds among the wheat.

Baptism

In the last chapter, *Epistles vs. Epistles*, it was noted that the Epistles do not address whether there's a baptism of the Spirit distinct from a baptism with water, whether baptism is only for repentance, or whether baptism is required for salvation: the Gospels and Acts do address these questions:

> *He (John) went throughout (the) whole region of the Jordan, proclaiming a baptism of repentance for the forgiveness of sins.*
> (Luke 3:3)

> *And this is what he (John) proclaimed: "One mightier than I is coming after me. I am not worthy to stoop and loosen the thongs of his sandals. I have baptized you with water; he will baptize you with the holy Spirit." It happened in those days that Jesus came from Nazareth of Galilee and was baptized in the Jordan by John.*
> (Mark 1:7-9; also Matthew 3:11, Luke 3:16, and John 1:26-27)

> *Then Jesus came from Galilee to John at the Jordan to be baptized by him. John tried to prevent him, saying, "I need to be baptized by you, and yet you are coming to me?" Jesus said to him in reply, "Allow it now, for thus it is fitting for us to fulfill all righteousness." Then he allowed him. After Jesus was baptized, he came up from the water and behold, the heavens were opened (for him), and he saw the Spirit of God descending like a dove (and) coming upon him.*
> (Matthew 3:13-16)

> *After all the people had been baptized and Jesus also had been baptized and was praying, heaven was opened and the holy Spirit descended upon him in bodily form like a dove. And a voice came from heaven, "You are my beloved Son; with you I am well pleased."*
> (Luke 3:21-22)

> *Now when Jesus learned that the Pharisees had heard that Jesus was making and baptizing more disciples than John (although Jesus himself was not baptizing, just his disciples), he left Judea and returned to Galilee*
> (John 4:1-3).

"I have come to set the earth on fire, and how I wish it were already blazing! There is a baptism with which I must be baptized, and how great is my anguish until it is accomplished!
(Luke 12:49-50)

––––––––

When the time for Pentecost was fulfilled, they were all in one place together. And suddenly there came from the sky a noise like a strong driving wind, and it filled the entire house in which they were. Then there appeared to them tongues as of fire, which parted and came to rest on each one of them. And they were all filled with the holy Spirit and began to speak in different tongues, as the Spirit enabled them to proclaim.
(Acts 2:1-4)

He said to them, "Go into the whole world and proclaim the gospel to every creature. Whoever believes and is baptized will be saved; whoever does not believe will be condemned.
(Mark 16:15-16)

"All power in heaven and on earth has been given to me. Go, therefore, and make disciples of all nations, baptizing them in the name of the Father, and of the Son, and of the holy Spirit, teaching them to observe all that I have commanded you. And behold, I am with you always, until the end of the age."
(Matthew 28:18-20)

––––––––

A Jew named Apollos, a native of Alexandria, an eloquent speaker, arrived in Ephesus. He was an authority on the scriptures. He had been instructed in the Way of the Lord and, with ardent spirit, spoke and taught accurately about Jesus, although he knew only the baptism of John. He began to speak boldly in the synagogue; but when Priscilla and Aquila heard him, they took him aside and explained to him the Way (of God) more accurately.
(Acts 18:24-26)

While Apollos was in Corinth, Paul traveled through the interior of the country and came (down) to Ephesus where he found some disciples. He said to them, "Did you receive the holy Spirit when you became believers?" They answered him, "We have never even heard that there is a holy Spirit." He said, "How were you baptized?" They replied, "With the baptism of John." Paul then said, "John baptized with a baptism of repentance, telling the people to believe in the one who was to come after him, that

is, in Jesus." When they heard this, they were baptized in the name of the Lord Jesus. And when Paul laid (his) hands on them, the holy Spirit came upon them, and they spoke in tongues and prophesied.
(Acts 19:1-6)

While the Gospels and Acts provide this additional information about Baptism and make it clear there are *two* baptisms, one with water for repentance, and one through the Holy Spirit, other questions are left unanswered: if baptism by the Holy Spirit did not occur until after Jesus' resurrection and Pentecost, were the baptisms that Jesus' followers performed prior to that also baptisms for repentance, as were John's? Did all those who had been baptized by water need to be re-baptized by the Spirit? If speaking in tongues is a definitive mark of baptism by the Holy Spirit, why doesn't that occur today except in fundamentalist sects? Is the physical act of baptism "magical" in that it requires no knowledge or understanding of the act, as in infant baptism, or does it require understanding and assent, as in adult baptism? And is the physical act of baptism required for salvation, as stated in Mark 16 but not elsewhere?

All of these open questions once again invite the hand of Man to choose preferred verses, fill in blanks, gloss over discrepancies, weave doctrines ... and fight among ourselves.

The Last Supper

As described in *Epistles vs. Epistles*, the only references to the Last Supper in the Epistles are in Paul's first letter to the Corinthians:

The cup of blessing that we bless, is it not a participation in the blood of Christ? The bread that we break, is it not a participation in the body of Christ? Because the loaf of bread is one, we, though many, are one body, for we all partake of the one loaf.
(1 Corinthians 10:16-17)

For I received from the Lord what I also handed on to you, that the Lord Jesus, on the night he was handed over, took bread, and, after he had given thanks, broke it and said, "This is my body that is for you. Do this in remembrance of me." In the same way also the cup, after supper, saying, "This cup is the

new covenant in my blood. Do this, as often as you drink it, in remembrance of me." For as often as you eat this bread and drink the cup, you proclaim the death of the Lord until he comes. Therefore whoever eats the bread or drinks the cup of the Lord unworthily will have to answer for the body and blood of the Lord.
(1 Corinthians 11:23-27)

The Gospels of Mark, Matthew, and Luke repeat Paul's First Corinthians 11 description almost word for word; only Luke, however, records Jesus as saying, "Do this in memory of me," corresponding to Paul's, "Do this in remembrance of me."

While they were eating, he took bread, said the blessing, broke it, and gave it to them, and said, "Take it; this is my body." Then he took a cup, gave thanks, and gave it to them, and they all drank from it. He said to them, "This is my blood of the covenant, which will be shed for many."
(Mark 14:22-24)

While they were eating, Jesus took bread, said the blessing, broke it, and giving it to his disciples said, "Take and eat; this is my body." Then he took a cup, gave thanks, and gave it to them, saying, "Drink from it, all of you, for this is my blood of the covenant, which will be shed on behalf of many for the forgiveness of sins"
(Matt 26:26-28)

He said to them, "I have eagerly desired to eat this Passover with you before I suffer, for, I tell you, I shall not eat it (again) until there is fulfillment in the kingdom of God." Then he took a cup, gave thanks, and said, "Take this and share it among yourselves; for I tell you (that) from this time on I shall not drink of the fruit of the vine until the kingdom of God comes." Then he took the bread, said the blessing, broke it, and gave it to them, saying, "This is my body, which will be given for you; do this in memory of me." And likewise the cup after they had eaten, saying, "This cup is the new covenant in my blood, which will be shed for you."
(Luke 22:15-20)

The Gospel of John contains no portrayal of a "last supper," but instead describes Jesus proclaiming a similar teaching in a different setting:

"I am the living bread that came down from heaven; whoever eats this bread will live forever; and the bread that I will give is

my flesh for the life of the world." The Jews quarreled among themselves, saying, "How can this man give us (his) flesh to eat?" Jesus said to them, "Amen, amen, I say to you, unless you eat the flesh of the Son of Man and drink his blood, you do not have life within you. Whoever eats my flesh and drinks my blood has eternal life, and I will raise him on the last day. For my flesh is true food, and my blood is true drink. Whoever eats my flesh and drinks my blood remains in me and I in him.
(John 6:51-56)

As with Paul's letter to the Corinthians, the Gospels do *not* state unambiguously whether Jesus meant "this is my body" and "this is my blood" symbolically, and only wanted future "Last Suppers" to be memorials to his sacrifice, or whether he meant the words literally and was proclaiming that future "Last Suppers" would be reenactments of his sacrifice. First Corinthians and the Gospels can be interpreted either way, and Christianity has for centuries divided itself on this issue alone. The fault, however, is not in the ambiguities of Scripture, but in our tribal animal insistence that our interpretation is true and other interpretations false, and in our compulsion to fight over differences rather than loving one another, as God loves us. … The fault, dear Theophilus, lies not in our scripture, but in ourselves.

⚜

In the next chapter, Chapter 10, *Epistles vs. Gospels*, we will look at how differences between the Epistles and the Gospels provide yet another opportunity for our tribal nature to turn differences into "weeds."

In Chapter 13, *What Jesus Did and Did Not Teach*, we will examine the Gospel teachings once again, this time using the *Sieve of the Spokesmen* to recognize Man's self-serving weeds scattered among the wheat – the bread of life – of Jesus' teachings.

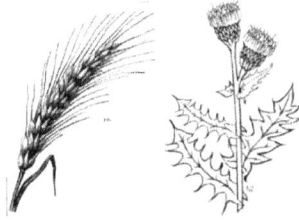

Chapter 10.
Epistles vs. Gospels

It should be apparent by now that our human nature allows us to harbor conflicting beliefs with little concern about the conflicts; we simply assume the differing beliefs complement rather than contradict, and effortlessly merge them in our minds. Our uncritical acceptance of the incompatible birth narratives in Matthew and Luke and the differences between the Synoptics and the Gospel of John demonstrates this well.

Similarly, it does not bother us that the Epistles and Gospels differ markedly in their representation of both Jesus and the means of salvation: the Gospels emphasize Jesus' teachings, his Jewish messiahship, and the need of both repentance and belief in him to be saved; the Epistles contain little of Jesus' teachings, identify Jesus as the transcendent Son of God who died for the sins of all, and maintain that all who believe in him are saved "by faith alone." The Gospels contain almost nothing suggesting an existing church hierarchy or developed doctrines, while the Epistles contain requirements and instructions for "presbyters" and "bishops," and contain doctrinal teachings on salvation, the second coming, and resurrection of the dead. There is also a difference between their teachings on forgiveness: in the Gospels Jesus tells us that God's forgiving us depends upon our forgiving others ...

> ... for if you forgive others their transgressions, your heavenly Father will forgive you. But if you do not forgive others, neither will your Father forgive your transgressions.
> (Matthew 6:12-15)

... but in the Epistles Paul tells us that believers are already forgiven, and because of this we should forgive others ...

> Be kind to one another, compassionate, forgiving one another as God has forgiven you in Christ.
> (Ephesians 4.32).

Because of these and other significant differences, it is possible to derive two very different "Christianities," one emphasizing Jesus' teachings in the Gospels, and the other emphasizing Jesus' ultimate triumph as described in the Epistles. Some Christian denominations/non-denominations emphasize one of these views to the exclusion of the other, some see them as complementary, but most profess some form of the view that the Gospels record Jesus' ministry as understood by his Jewish followers (with just the beginning of an awareness of his larger mission), and the Epistles record and expound Jesus' larger mission, as ecstatically revealed to Paul by the transformed Jesus. ... In this latter view the Epistles do not "complement" the Gospels, but complete our understanding of them.

This break between the Epistles and Gospels is not "clean," however, for both contain verses reflecting the prevailing views of the other. For example, Paul's First Corinthians' description of the Last Supper is included almost word for word in the Gospel of Mark, and despite the Epistles' emphasis on "faith alone," they nonetheless record:

> For we must all appear before the judgment seat of Christ, so that each one may receive recompense, according to what he did in the body, whether good or evil.
> (2 Corinthians 5:10)

and:

> What good is it, my brothers, if someone says he has faith but does not have works? Can that faith save him?
> (James 2:14)

Scholars attempting to understand the differences between the Gospels and the Epistles suggest they reflect differences between the "*Jewish* Christian" communities and "*Gentile*

Christian" communities that coexisted from Jesus' ascension until the destruction of Jerusalem and the final dispersion of Judaism. Thanks to the preservation of the Epistles, we have source material from the *Gentile* Christian communities during this approximately forty year period, but we have no comparable source material from the *Jewish* Christian communities. If any comparable documents ever existed they have not survived, so all that can be known about the Jewish Christian community from 30 C.E. to 70 C.E. must be gleaned or inferred from excerpts from Paul's letters, the Book of Acts, the Sayings Gospel Q (imbedded in Matthew and Luke), and surviving extra-Biblical sources.

This gap in the historical record can be disconcerting. If someone who has already read the Gospel of Mark reads Acts for the first time, they will likely be startled to find that James, the brother of Jesus who was last seen with his family questioning Jesus' sanity in the Gospel of Mark, is now the leader – the leader! – of a Jerusalem (not Nazareth or Capernaum) Christian enclave that includes Peter, and James and John the sons of Zebedee. This remarkable turnaround is not explained in Scripture, but extra-Biblical writings by early church leaders and historians record that James the brother of Jesus, called "James the Just" because of his righteousness, was named a bishop of Jerusalem by the Apostles and was their leader for thirty years. ... This striking example should alert us that significant information we would like to know about Jewish Christianity between 30 and 70 C.E. is not recorded in Scripture.

The authentic letters of Paul (those agreed to have actually been written by Paul) and the Book of Acts do, however, provide a means of gleaning information about the Jewish Christian community by observing Paul's interaction with them as recorded in those documents. This should be done cautiously, for Paul's letters present only *Paul's* side of the agreements and disagreements between himself and the Jewish Christian community, and the Book of Acts, written decades later, sometimes disagrees factually with what Paul wrote. For example, in his letter to the Galatians Paul strongly emphasized that following his conversion he did *not* go to Jerusalem or the disciples for instruction:

> Now I want you to know, brothers, that the gospel preached by me is not of human origin. For I did not receive it from a human being, nor was I taught it, but it came through a revelation of Jesus Christ. ... I did not immediately consult flesh and blood, nor did I go up to Jerusalem to those who were apostles before me; rather, I went into Arabia and then returned to Damascus. Then after three years I went up to Jerusalem to confer with Cephas and remained with him for fifteen days. But I did not see any other of the apostles, only James the brother of the Lord. ... Then I went into the regions of Syria and Cilicia.
> (1Galatians 1:11-21)

Acts, however, contains three conflicting narratives all indicating in differing ways that Paul *did* go to Jerusalem following his conversion:

> He stayed some days with the disciples in Damascus, and he began at once to proclaim Jesus in the synagogues, that he is the Son of God. .... After a long time had passed, the Jews conspired to kill him ... but his disciples took him one night and let him down through an opening in the wall, lowering him in a basket. When he arrived in Jerusalem he tried to join the disciples, but they were all afraid of him, not believing that he was a disciple.
> (Acts 9:19-26)

> A certain Ananias, a devout observer of the law, and highly spoken of by all the Jews who lived there, came to me and stood there and said, 'Saul, my brother, regain your sight.' And at that very moment I regained my sight and saw him. Then he said ... Get up and have yourself baptized and your sins washed away, calling upon his name.' After I had returned to Jerusalem and while I was praying in the temple, I fell into a trance and saw the Lord saying to me, 'Hurry, leave Jerusalem at once, because they will not accept your testimony about me.'
> (Acts 22:12-18)

> And the Lord replied, 'I am Jesus whom you are persecuting. ... I have appeared to you for this purpose, to appoint you as a servant and witness of what you have seen (of me) and what you will be shown. ... I was not disobedient to the heavenly

vision. On the contrary, first to those in Damascus and in Jerusalem and throughout the whole country of Judea, and then to the Gentiles, I preached the need to repent and turn to God, and to do works giving evidence of repentance.
(Acts 26:15-20)

Since the author of Luke-Acts describes himself as *"investigating everything accurately anew ... so that you may realize the certainty of the teachings you have received,"* it seems surprising that he could be unaware of Paul's letter to the Galatians, but that appears to be the case. ... It's equally surprising that he could provide three differing narratives of Paul's conversion without commenting on the discrepancies, but again, that is the case. When faced with conflicts such as these between Paul's own words and words written about him decades later, scholars generally weight Paul's words more than the latter.

Because Paul's letters were written in the 50's and 60's and the Gospels not until the 70's to 100's, it is reasonable and natural to wonder how much Paul's letters influenced the later writing of the Gospels. ... Observing that Mark embeds Paul's description of the Last Supper, is it likely this was the one and only time Paul's writings influenced the Gospels? ... Massive scholarship has been devoted toward detecting knowledge of Paul's letters and/or thinking within the Gospels, and massive disagreement has been the result: some scholars claim the pervasiveness of Paul's letters and thinking so influenced the writing of Gospels-Acts that they are essentially Pauline documents; some claim Paul's influence on the Gospels was minimal to non-existent; and others fall between these extremes. For Christians (as opposed to Biblical scholars) who believe Paul's teachings came directly from the transformed Jesus and completed a full understanding of Jesus' mission, the possibility of Pauline influence on the Gospels is of no concern.

In spite of possible influences by Paul, the *Jewish* Christian understanding of Jesus' role and teachings became dominant in the Gospels due to the embedding of the Sayings Gospel Q in Matthew and Luke. As described in the previous chapter, the

Sayings Gospel Q is a collection of Jesus' teachings that was passed on orally (or perhaps written down but lost) by his followers. As such it contains the core of his teachings with no accompanying narratives or theology, and is probably what the Jewish Christian community continued to teach in the years following his ascension … what James the Just, Peter, and James and John the sons of Zebedee taught in Jerusalem and Judea until the destruction and exile.

≈

Although the differences between the Gospels and Epistles are treated as "weeds" by those wishing to diminish Judeo-Christianity, they are better seen as evidence of the Spirit drawing people from all human starting points toward a more perfect understanding of God working through Jesus for our salvation. … As in Roman's 8:28, "*We know that all things work for good for those who love God, who are called according to his purpose*." As much now as in the first century C.E., we continually struggle with the battles between *the Flesh* and *the Spirit*, and the teachings of Jesus and Paul combine to guide us in our struggles.

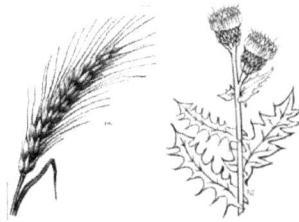

Chapter 11.
The Jewish Diversion

I use the term "The Jewish Diversion" to refer to the combined phenomena of:

1) the Gospels transitioning from condemning *religious leaders and practices* to condemning *"the Jews;"*

2) the Epistles using Jewish-specific titles that allow misidentifying *human* failings as *Jewish* failings.

It is impossible to lament these two phenomena adequately. Rather than being merely "weeds among the wheat," these self-serving distortions of Jesus' and Paul's teachings are more like invading kudzu ... they exploit our tribal desire for a scapegoat enemy, and have been the direct cause of Christianity's two thousand years of enmity toward Judaism and the incalculable suffering accompanying it.

❧

Consider first the phenomenon of the Gospels' transitioning from condemning Jewish *religious leaders and practices* to condemning *"the Jews."*

In the earliest Gospel, the Gospel of Mark, the antagonism of the Priests, Scribes, Pharisees, and Sadducees toward Jesus and Jesus' reaction to it is described with minimal polemics by simply describing their words, intents, and actions.

Now when the Pharisees with some scribes who had come from Jerusalem gathered around him, they observed that some of his disciples ate their meals with unclean, that is, unwashed,

hands. (For the Pharisees and, in fact, all Jews, do not eat without carefully washing their hands, keeping the tradition of the elders. And on coming from the marketplace they do not eat without purifying themselves. And there are many other things that they have traditionally observed, the purification of cups and jugs and kettles [and beds].) So the Pharisees and scribes questioned him, "Why do your disciples not follow the tradition of the elders but instead eat a meal with unclean hands?" He responded, "Well did Isaiah prophesy about you hypocrites, as it is written: 'This people honors me with their lips, but their hearts are far from me; In vain do they worship me, teaching as doctrines human precepts.' You disregard God's commandment but cling to human tradition." He went on to say, "How well you have set aside the commandment of God in order to uphold your tradition! For Moses said, 'Honor your father and your mother,' and 'Whoever curses father or mother shall die.' Yet you say, 'If a person says to father or mother, "Any support you might have had from me is qorban"' (meaning, dedicated to God), you allow him to do nothing more for his father or mother. You nullify the word of God in favor of your tradition that you have handed on. And you do many such things."
(Mark 7:1-13)

In the course of his teaching he said, "Beware of the scribes, who like to go around in long robes and accept greetings in the marketplaces, seats of honor in synagogues, and places of honor at banquets. They devour the houses of widows and, as a pretext, recite lengthy prayers. They will receive a very severe condemnation."
(Mark 12:38-40)

In the Gospels of Matthew and Luke, however, Jesus is shown responding to the antagonism of the religious leaders with harsh condemnation:

Jesus spoke to the crowds and to his disciples, saying, "The scribes and the Pharisees have taken their seat on the chair of Moses. Therefore, do and observe all things whatsoever they tell you, but do not follow their example. For they preach but they do not practice. They tie up heavy burdens (hard to carry) and lay them on people's shoulders, but they will not lift a finger to move them. All their works are performed to be seen. They widen their phylacteries and lengthen their tassels. They love places of honor at banquets, seats of honor in synagogues, greetings in

marketplaces, and the salutation 'Rabbi.' ... "Woe to you, scribes and Pharisees, you hypocrites. You lock the kingdom of heaven before human beings. You do not enter yourselves, nor do you allow entrance to those trying to enter. "Woe to you, scribes and Pharisees, you hypocrites. You traverse sea and land to make one convert, and when that happens you make him a child of Gehenna twice as much as yourselves. "Woe to you, blind guides, who say, 'If one swears by the temple, it means nothing, but if one swears by the gold of the temple, one is obligated.' Blind fools, which is greater, the gold, or the temple that made the gold sacred? And you say, 'If one swears by the altar, it means nothing, but if one swears by the gift on the altar, one is obligated.' You blind ones, which is greater, the gift, or the altar that makes the gift sacred? One who swears by the altar swears by it and all that is upon it; one who swears by the temple swears by it and by him who dwells in it; one who swears by heaven swears by the throne of God and by him who is seated on it. "Woe to you, scribes and Pharisees, you hypocrites. You pay tithes of mint and dill and cummin, and have neglected the weightier things of the law: judgment and mercy and fidelity. (But) these you should have done, without neglecting the others. Blind guides, who strain out the gnat and swallow the camel! "Woe to you, scribes and Pharisees, you hypocrites. You cleanse the outside of cup and dish, but inside they are full of plunder and self-indulgence. Blind Pharisee, cleanse first the inside of the cup, so that the outside also may be clean. "Woe to you, scribes and Pharisees, you hypocrites. You are like whitewashed tombs, which appear beautiful on the outside, but inside are full of dead men's bones and every kind of filth. Even so, on the outside you appear righteous, but inside you are filled with hypocrisy and evildoing. "Woe to you, scribes and Pharisees, you hypocrites. You build the tombs of the prophets and adorn the memorials of the righteous, and you say, 'If we had lived in the days of our ancestors, we would not have joined them in shedding the prophets' blood.' Thus you bear witness against yourselves that you are the children of those who murdered the prophets; now fill up what your ancestors measured out! You serpents, you brood of vipers, how can you flee from the judgment of Gehenna?
(Matthew 23:1-33)

After he had spoken, a Pharisee invited him to dine at his home. He entered and reclined at table to eat. The Pharisee was amazed to see that he did not observe the prescribed washing

before the meal. The Lord said to him, "Oh you Pharisees! Although you cleanse the outside of the cup and the dish, inside you are filled with plunder and evil. You fools! Did not the maker of the outside also make the inside? But as to what is within, give alms, and behold, everything will be clean for you. Woe to you Pharisees! You pay tithes of mint and of rue and of every garden herb, but you pay no attention to judgment and to love for God. These you should have done, without overlooking the others. Woe to you Pharisees! You love the seat of honor in synagogues and greetings in marketplaces. Woe to you! You are like unseen graves over which people unknowingly walk." Then one of the scholars of the law said to him in reply, "Teacher, by saying this you are insulting us too." And he said, "Woe also to you scholars of the law! You impose on people burdens hard to carry, but you yourselves do not lift one finger to touch them. Woe to you! You build the memorials of the prophets whom your ancestors killed. Consequently, you bear witness and give consent to the deeds of your ancestors, for they killed them and you do the building. Therefore, the wisdom of God said, 'I will send to them prophets and apostles; some of them they will kill and persecute' in order that this generation might be charged with the blood of all the prophets shed since the foundation of the world, from the blood of Abel to the blood of Zechariah who died between the altar and the temple building. Yes, I tell you, this generation will be charged with their blood! Woe to you, scholars of the law! You have taken away the key of knowledge. You yourselves did not enter and you stopped those trying to enter." When he left, the scribes and Pharisees began to act with hostility toward him and to interrogate him about many things, for they were plotting to catch him at something he might say.
(Luke 11:37-54)

In the last Gospel, the Gospel of John, Jesus' harsh condemnation of religious leaders and their practices is recast as a condemnation of "*the Jews*," as if Jesus and his followers weren't Jews!

Since the Passover of the Jews was near, Jesus went up to Jerusalem.
(John 2:13)

The man went and told the Jews that Jesus was the one who had made him well. Therefore, the Jews began to persecute Jesus because he did this on a sabbath. But Jesus answered

them, "My Father is at work until now, so I am at work." For this reason the Jews tried all the more to kill him, because he not only broke the sabbath but he also called God his own father, making himself equal to God.
(John 5:15-18)

After this, Jesus moved about within Galilee; but he did not wish to travel in Judea, because the Jews were trying to kill him.
(John 7:1)

(So) the Jews said to him, "Now we are sure that you are possessed. Abraham died, as did the prophets, yet you say, 'Whoever keeps my word will never taste death.' Are you greater than our father Abraham, who died? Or the prophets, who died? Who do you make yourself out to be?"
(John 8:52-53)

The Jews again picked up rocks to stone him. Jesus answered them, "I have shown you many good works from my Father. For which of these are you trying to stone me?" The Jews answered him, "We are not stoning you for a good work but for blasphemy. You, a man, are making yourself God."
(John 10:31-33)

My children, I will be with you only a little while longer. You will look for me, and as I told the Jews, 'Where I go you cannot come,' so now I say it to you.
(John 13:33-33)

The high priest questioned Jesus about his disciples and about his doctrine. Jesus answered him, "I have spoken publicly to the world. I have always taught in a synagogue or in the temple area where all the Jews gather, and in secret I have said nothing.
(John 18:19-20)

It is generally accepted that the cause of this increasingly antagonistic rhetoric toward Judaism was the growing separation between the Gentile Christian communities and the Jewish Christian communities. Paul's letter to the Galatians and the Book of Acts both record that the Jerusalem Council ($\approx$ 50 C.E.) agreed Paul should witness to the Gentiles and that Gentiles would not be required to be circumcised ... but they also record that this agreement was not strictly adhered to by either side. Paul typically preached first in Jewish synagogues, raising concerns in Jerusalem that he was teaching that *Jews* need not adhere to the Mosaic Law, and Jewish Christians traveled from Jerusalem to Paul's Gentile communities to try to convince them that circumcision *was* required. Paul's letters to the Corinthians, Galatians, and Philippians reveal the bitterness of his feelings about the latter, and it was to answer charges about the former that he returned to Jerusalem and was imprisoned.

⚚

Consider next the second phenomenon contributing to the Jewish Diversion … the Epistles' use of Jewish-specific language that allows misidentifying *human* failings as *Jewish* failings.

Imagine yourself a high school Physics student required to conduct an "inclined-plane" experiment. You are given a variety of white spherical objects and black egg-shaped objects, and instructed to roll them down a ramp and draw conclusions from what you observe. After completing the experiment you triumphantly conclude, "White objects roll faster than black objects!", foolishly imagining that the significant factor was the *color* rather than the *shape*.

You laugh at this anecdote, certain that no one would ever make such an egregious misinterpretation of observed data, but that is exactly what (we) Christians have done with Jesus' teachings against Jewish religious leaders and their practices. We have foolishly concluded the significant factor was their being *Jewish* (their "color") rather than being *human religious leaders* (their "shape"), and by doing so we have allowed Christianity to unwittingly fall prey to the same faults.

For example, Jesus taught …

"This people honors me with their lips, but their hearts are far from me; In vain do they worship me, teaching as doctrines human precepts. You disregard God's commandment but cling to human tradition."
(Mark 7:6-8, quoting Isaiah 29:13)

... and to illustrate this, Jesus pointed out that the Law of Moses required honoring your father and mother, but the Pharisees allowed a tradition of telling your father and mother that "any support you might have had from me is dedicated to God," and thus to not honor or support them. ... Correspondingly, Jesus taught in the Gospel of John that he wanted his followers "to be one" that the world might believe, but Christian "Pharisees" have allowed a tradition of honoring their divisive doctrines rather than obeying Jesus' injunction "to be one."

Jesus also taught ...

"Woe to you scholars of the law! You impose on people burdens hard to carry, but you yourselves do not lift one finger to touch them.
(Luke 11:46)

The burdens the Jewish scholars of the law (Scribes) imposed were the many ancillary "teachings of men" they proudly saw as "building a fence around the Torah" to protect it from accidental violation. The burdens Christian scholars of the law (Theologians) proudly impose are the many nuanced doctrines and sacraments dividing Christianity into feudal denominations and non-denominations.

It's easy to understand how Christianity became deceived into believing Jesus' teachings were directed against *Jewish* flaws rather than *human* flaws. First, our tribal nature makes us predisposed to seek a "scapegoat enemy" tribe to blame for all evils; and Second, the New Testament uses Jewish-specific titles for the various religious groups, (subtribes) that are common to most religions. To see beneath the labels and experience the significance of Jesus' and Paul's teachings, it is necessary to mentally replace the Jewish-specific labels with Christian equivalents, as in the following table:

When reading …	Substitute …
Jews, Jewish	Christians, Christian
Scribes, Teachers of the Law	Theologians
Chief Priests	Ranking Clergy
Priests	Low-level Clergy
Levites	Congregational Staff
Pharisees, Sadducees	Committed, regular worshippers and/or those serving on congregational governing bodies
People of the Land	People who don't worship regularly
Samaritan	Least-liked other religions
Gentiles	Un-believers
Circumcision	Baptism
Law	Gospel
Teachings of Men	Doctrines, Sacraments

See how more meaningful to us Paul's letter to the Romans becomes when we make these substitutions:

For God does not show favoritism. All who disobey his will apart from the gospel will also perish apart from the gospel, and all who sin under the gospel will be judged by the gospel. For it is not those who hear the gospel who are righteous in God's sight, but it is those who do his will who will be declared righteous. Indeed, when non-believers, who do not have the gospel, do by nature things required by the gospel, they are a gospel for themselves, even though they do not have the gospel, since they show that the requirements of the gospel are written on their hearts, their consciences also bearing witness, and their thoughts now accusing, now even defending them.
(Romans 2:11-15)

You who brag about the Gospel, do you dishonor God by not doing his will? As it is written: "God's name is blasphemed among the un-believers because of you." Baptism has value if you obey God's will, but if you do not obey God's will, you have become as though you had not been baptized. If those who are not baptized do God's will, will they not be regarded as though they were baptized? The one who is not baptized physically and yet does God's will condemns you who, even though you have the gospels and baptism, do not obey. A man is not a Christian if he is only one outwardly, nor is baptism merely outward and

physical. No, a man is a Christian if he is one inwardly; and baptism is baptism of the heart, by the Spirit, not by the physical act. Such a man's praise is not from men, but from God.
(Romans 2:23-29)

For we maintain that a man is justified by faith apart from observing the gospel. Is God the God of Christians only? Is he not the God of non-believers too? Yes, of non-believers too, since there is only one God, who will justify the baptized by faith and the unbaptized through that same faith.
(Romans 3:28-30)

Although it is disconcerting to read these passages as being directed at Christians (us) and our (blind?) devotion to the Gospel and baptism rather than at Jews and their blind devotion to the Law and circumcision, it is only by doing this that we can overcome the "Jewish Diversion" and gain greater insight into New Testament teachings.

⋐∾⋑

In the Gospels it is recorded that Jesus' contemporaries sometimes identified him as a prophet. In the next chapter we'll examine the ways in which Jesus was like and unlike the Jewish Reform Prophets.

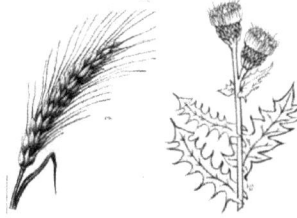

Chapter 12.
Jesus as Reform Prophet

While it has traditionally been acknowledged that Jesus of Nazareth fulfilled the roles of both Jewish prophet and teacher ...

Others were saying, "He is Elijah"; still others, "He is a prophet like any of the prophets."
(Mark 6:15)

Then some of the scribes and Pharisees said to him, "Teacher, we wish to see a sign from you."
(Matthew 12:38)

... the desire to spread awareness of Jesus as the Jewish Messiah and the Son of God has caused Christians to oppose discussing him as a "mere" prophet, religious reformer, or teacher.

This is regrettable for four reasons:

First, discouraging discussion of Jesus as a prophet, teacher, or reformer scorches what could be common ground with Judaism, Islam and Secularism. ... If Jesus' teachings are worthwhile for the world, would it not be better for them to be promulgated, appreciated, and lived-by rather than husbanded as a preserve accessible only to Christians? ... If they are true, and make the world a better place to live when practiced, shouldn't they be freely shared whether the world considers Jesus the Son of God or not?

Second, by not relating Jesus to the Reform Prophets a significant theological thread linking the Old and New Testaments – the recurring need to reform corrupt religious practices – is overlooked.

Third, recognizing that Jesus addressed the same problems as the Reform Prophets demonstrates how unchanging human nature is, and how our persistent flaws have had to be addressed repeatedly throughout Scripture.

Fourth, acknowledging Jesus and the Reform Prophets as reformers of religion draws attention to the many ways religions become corrupt, and encourages examining what doctrines and practices of religion need reform today.

挃

Chapter 5, *Prophets and Spokesmen*, reviewed the major themes of the Reform Prophets and used representative quotes to show that their teachings consistently emphasized the then radical view that:

- Love for fellowman is equivalent to love for God;
- Religious observances not arising from an underlying love of God and fellowman are meaningless.

The implication of these intertwined themes is that true religion is measured by inner attitudes that result in outer actions, rather than the by the outer actions themselves.

Despite the vastly different circumstances between when the Reform Prophets wrote and when Jesus spoke – between being threatened with extinction by the Assyrians and Babylonians in the 8th century B.C.E, and being a conquered, occupied vassal state of Rome in the 1st century C.E. – Jesus' teachings addressed nearly all of the major themes of the Reform Prophets and greatly expanded on the importance of inner attitudes. Here are representative quotes by Jesus on Reform Prophet themes:

The nation is morally corrupt: it does not obey God

"Woe to you, Chorazin! Woe to you, Bethsaida! For if the mighty deeds done in your midst had been done in Tyre and Sidon, they would long ago have repented in sackcloth and ashes. But I tell you, it will be more tolerable for Tyre and Sidon on the day of judgment than for you. And as for you, Capernaum: 'Will you be exalted to heaven? You will go down to the netherworld. 'For if the mighty deeds done in your midst had been done in Sodom, it would have remained until this day. But I tell you, it will be more tolerable for the land of Sodom on the day of judgment than for you."
(Matt 11:21-24)

The nation's leaders allow social injustice

"Woe to you, scribes and Pharisees, you hypocrites. You pay tithes of mint and dill and cummin, and have neglected the weightier things of the law: judgment and mercy and fidelity. (But) these you should have done, without neglecting the others. ... "Woe to you, scribes and Pharisees, you hypocrites. You cleanse the outside of cup and dish, but inside they are full of plunder and self-indulgence.
(Matt 23:23-25)

Disaster will befall the nation unless it repents

"When you see the desolating abomination spoken of through Daniel the prophet standing in the holy place (let the reader understand), then those in Judea must flee to the mountains, a person on the housetop must not go down to get things out of his house, a person in the field must not return to get his cloak. Woe to pregnant women and nursing mothers in those days. Pray that your flight not be in winter or on the sabbath, for at that time there will be great tribulation, such as has not been since the beginning of the world until now, nor ever will be.
(Matt 24:15-21)

False Priests and Prophets lead the people astray.

Woe to you scribes and Pharisees, you frauds! You shut the doors of the kingdom of God in men's faces, neither entering yourselves nor admitting those who are trying to enter. Woe to you scribes and Pharisees, you frauds! You travel over sea and land to make a convert, but once he is converted you make a devil of him twice as wicked as yourselves. It is an evil day for you, blind guides! ... Woe to you scribes and Pharisees, you frauds! You pay tithes on mint and herbs and seeds while

neglecting the weightier matters of the law, justice and mercy and good faith. It is these you should have practiced, without neglecting the others. Blind guides! You strain out the gnat and swallow the camel! Woe to you, scribes and Pharisees, you frauds! You cleanse the outside of cup and dish, and leave the inside filled with loot and lust! Blind Pharisee! First cleanse the inside of the cup so that its outside may be clean.
(Matt 23:13-16, 23-27)

Worshipping man-made idols or other gods is foolish and abominable
(Not addressed by Jesus)

The "Day of the Lord" will bring judgment, not reward
"Not everyone who says to me, 'Lord, Lord,' will enter the kingdom of heaven, but only the one who does the will of my Father in heaven. Many will say to me on that day, 'Lord, Lord, did we not prophesy in your name? Did we not drive out demons in your name? Did we not do mighty deeds in your name?' Then I will declare to them solemnly, 'I never knew you. Depart from me, you evildoers.'
(Matt 7:21-23)

God uses other nations to punish Israel;
(Not addressed by Jesus)

A faithful remnant will survive
Many false prophets will arise and deceive many; and because of the increase of evildoing, the love of many will grow cold. But the one who perseveres to the end will be saved.
(Matt 24:11)

God will someday create a New Jerusalem, a perfect society
And then the sign of the Son of Man will appear in heaven, and all the tribes of the earth will mourn, and they will see the Son of Man coming upon the clouds of heaven with power and great glory. And he will send out his angels with a trumpet blast, and they will gather his elect from the four winds, from one end of the heavens to the other.
(Matt 24:30-31)

God is God of all the Nations, not just Israel
But a Samaritan who was journeying along came on him and was moved to pity at the sight. ... Which of these three, in your opinion, was neighbor to the man who fell in with the robbers?

The answer came, "The one who treated him with compassion."
Jesus said, "Then go and do the same."
(Luke 10:33, 36-37)

All nations will eventually turn to the God of Zion

And this gospel of the kingdom will be preached throughout the
world as a witness to all nations, and then the end will come.
(Matt 24:14)

Individuals are responsible only for their own sins, not "sons for the sins of their fathers"

(Not addressed by Jesus)

"Teachings of men" distort God's will for Man

So the Pharisees and scribes questioned him, "Why do your
disciples not follow the tradition of the elders but instead eat a
meal with unclean hands?" He responded, "Well did Isaiah
prophesy about you hypocrites, as it is written: 'This people
honors me with their lips, but their hearts are far from me; In vain
do they worship me, teaching as doctrines human precepts.' You
disregard God's commandment but cling to human tradition."
(Mark 7:5-7)

God wants caring for others, not religious rituals

He will put the sheep on his right and the goats on his left. "Then
the King will say to those on his right, 'Come, you who are
blessed by my Father; take your inheritance, the kingdom
prepared for you since the creation of the world. For I was
hungry and you gave me something to eat, I was thirsty and you
gave me something to drink, I was a stranger and you invited me
in, I needed clothes and you clothed me, I was sick and you
looked after me, I was in prison and you came to visit me.' "Then
the righteous will answer him, 'Lord, when did we see you
hungry and feed you, or thirsty and give you something to drink?
When did we see you a stranger and invite you in, or needing
clothes and clothe you? When did we see you sick or in prison
and go to visit you?' "The King will reply, 'I tell you the truth,
whatever you did for one of the least of these brothers of mine,
you did for me.'
(Matt 25:32-40)

These verses demonstrate that Jesus did indeed follow in the
footsteps of the Reform Prophets, for his teachings echoed and
amplified their teachings. Matthew even records that on two

occasions (Matt 9:13 and 12:7) Jesus specifically quoted Hosea's, "*I desire mercy, not sacrifice,*" to the Pharisees.

Jesus' teachings also make explicit the Reform Prophets' implicit recognition that "true religion is measured by inner attitudes rather than outer actions": he expressed it in many ways:

> "You have heard that it was said to your ancestors, 'You shall not kill; and whoever kills will be liable to judgment.' But I say to you, whoever is angry with his brother will be liable to judgment, and whoever says to his brother, 'Raqa,' will be answerable to the Sanhedrin, and whoever says, 'You fool,' will be liable to fiery Gehenna.
> (Matt 5:21-22)

> "You have heard that it was said, 'You shall not commit adultery.' But I say to you, everyone who looks at a woman with lust has already committed adultery with her in his heart.
> (Matt 5:27-28)

> While he was still speaking to the crowds, his mother and his brothers appeared outside, wishing to speak with him. (Someone told him, "Your mother and your brothers are standing outside, asking to speak with you.") But he said in reply to the one who told him, "Who is my mother? Who are my brothers?" And stretching out his hand toward his disciples, he said, "Here are my mother and my brothers. For whoever does the will of my heavenly Father is my brother, and sister, and mother."
> (Matt 12:46-50)

> Do you not realize that everything that enters the mouth passes into the stomach and is expelled into the latrine? But the things that come out of the mouth come from the heart, and they defile. For from the heart come evil thoughts, murder, adultery, unchastity, theft, false witness, blasphemy. These are what defile a person, but to eat with unwashed hands does not defile."
> (Matt 15:17-20)

> "Woe to you, blind guides, who say, 'If one swears by the temple, it means nothing, but if one swears by the gold of the temple, one is obligated.' Blind fools, which is greater, the gold, or the temple that made the gold sacred? And you say, 'If one swears by the altar, it means nothing, but if one swears by the gift on the altar, one is obligated.' You blind ones, which is greater, the gift, or the altar that makes the gift sacred?
> (Matt 23:16-19)

"Woe to you, scribes and Pharisees, you hypocrites. You cleanse the outside of cup and dish, but inside they are full of plunder and self-indulgence. Blind Pharisee, cleanse first the inside of the cup, so that the outside also may be clean. "Woe to you, scribes and Pharisees, you hypocrites. You are like whitewashed tombs, which appear beautiful on the outside, but inside are full of dead men's bones and every kind of filth. Even so, on the outside you appear righteous, but inside you are filled with hypocrisy and evildoing.
(Matt 23:25-28)

Through all of these examples Jesus taught that inner attitudes motivate outward behavior ... but it's taken till now, two thousand years later, for science to finally *prove* that underlying biases do indeed predispose and motivate our behavior.

While the nearly complete agreement of the teachings of Jesus with that of the Reform Prophets is clear, there is one significant difference that has been routinely overlooked: *Jesus did not demand social justice.* ... Instead, he instructed his followers (including us) how to respond to injustice. While the Prophets harangued the princes and rulers of Israel and Judah (as well as the religious leaders) for their social injustice ...

... your princes are rebels and comrades of thieves; each of them loves a bribe and looks for gifts ...
(Isaiah 1:23)

Woe to those who enact unjust statutes and who write oppressive decrees, depriving the needy of judgment and robbing my poor people of their rights, making widows their plunder, and orphans their prey!
(Isaiah 10:1-2)

Then I said, "Listen, you leaders of Jacob, you rulers of the house of Israel. Should you not know justice, you who hate good and love evil; who tear the skin from my people and the flesh from their bones?"
(Micah 3:1-2)

... the ruler demands gifts, the judge accepts bribes, the powerful dictate what they desire-- they all conspire together.
(Micah 7:3)

> For there are among my people criminals ... They go their
> wicked way; justice they do not defend by advancing the claims
> of the fatherless or judging the cause of the poor.
> (Jeremiah 5:26-28)

... Jesus spoke only against the *religious* leaders (the Priests, Scribes and Pharisees) and called for *religious reform* rather than *social reform*. Recognizing this is at first startling, for we are accustomed to uncritically assuming that Jesus, like the Prophets, called for social justice. The Gospels, however, record that rather than demanding social justice, Jesus instead taught how we as individuals should respond when we experience injustice; invariably he called upon us to reexamine our own position, our own inner attitudes:

> Why do you notice the splinter in your brother's eye, but do not
> perceive the wooden beam in your own eye? How can you say
> to your brother, 'Let me remove that splinter from your eye,'
> while the wooden beam is in your eye? You hypocrite, remove
> the wooden beam from your eye first; then you will see clearly to
> remove the splinter from your brother's eye.
> (Matt 7:3-5)

> As they continued their journey he entered a village where a
> woman whose name was Martha welcomed him. She had a
> sister named Mary (who) sat beside the Lord at his feet listening
> to him speak. Martha, burdened with much serving, came to him
> and said, "Lord, do you not care that my sister has left me by
> myself to do the serving? Tell her to help me." The Lord said to
> her in reply, "Martha, Martha, you are anxious and worried about
> many things. There is need of only one thing. Mary has chosen
> the better part and it will not be taken from her."
> (Luke 10:38-42)

> Someone in the crowd said to him, "Teacher, tell my brother to
> share the inheritance with me." He replied to him, "Friend, who
> appointed me as your judge and arbitrator?"
> (Luke 12:13-14)

> At that time the disciples approached Jesus and said, "Who is
> the greatest in the kingdom of heaven?" He called a child over,
> placed it in their midst, and said, "Amen, I say to you, unless you
> turn and become like children, you will not enter the kingdom of
> heaven. Whoever humbles himself like this child is the greatest

in the kingdom of heaven. And whoever receives one child such
as this in my name receives me.
(Matt 18:1-5)

With the new and growing awareness of our tribal human
nature, it is now possible to understand the wisdom of Jesus'
teachings: they strike directly at our tribal predisposition to see
other tribes – those having beliefs or opinions different from ours
– as enemies to be dominated rather than as fellow tribemembers,
children of the one God.

❦

While it has been uncomfortable considering the existence of
weeds among the wheat even in the New Testament, we are now,
finally, at the point where we can apply the *Sieve of the
Spokesmen* to the question of greatest importance to Christianity:
What Did and Didn't Jesus Teach?

By examining whether teachings attributed to Jesus honor
God and humble Man, or empower Man and diminish God we
will be able to detect which teachings are "wheat" and which are
"weeds" – which Jesus actually taught and which he almost
certainly did not. In the final chapter, Chapter 14, we can then
consider what Christianity *should* teach, so that Jesus' followers
might become one and the world might believe.

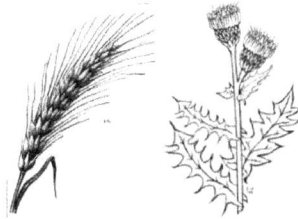

Chapter 13.
What Jesus Did and Didn't Teach

Jesus' teachings directly address Man's tribal flaws, especially our predisposition to favor our own tribe (and beliefs) over other tribes (and their beliefs.) This predisposition is not a "religious" predisposition but a human predisposition: we try to impose secular beliefs as enthusiastically and homicidally as we do religious beliefs (see Communism.) ... Religious tribal behavior is simply a particularly visible subset of Human tribal behavior. This instinct-driven tribal behavior causes us to be both "Good" and "Evil": good to those within our tribes but capable of utter evil to those without. It is these unconscious, powerfully motivating instincts that must be overcome if the human race is ever to "live in peace," and the teachings of Jesus provide the means of doing so.

Sadly, as we have seen, the teachings of Jesus recorded in the Gospels allow differing interpretations, and the differing interpretations give rise to the many denominations and non-denominations contending with one another rather than being witnesses to the world for Christ. This millennia-old tragedy will not, cannot, ever end until we accept the reality of our quarreling, compulsively warring tribal nature and admit that the doctrines we fight over are of no more importance to God than were the feasts, holocausts, and rituals of ancient Israel.

We also have seen that the teachings of Jesus recorded in the Gospels sometimes seem sufficiently at odds with themselves to raise the question, "Did Jesus actually teach this?" The challenge is to find a means of discerning which of the Gospels' teachings are God-inspired, to be lived by, and which are Man-influenced, to be recognized as such. The *"Sieve of the Spokesmen"* introduced in Chapter 5, *Prophets and Spokesmen*, provides such a means:

> *If a teaching gives glory to God,*
> *… showing him to be loving, just, and merciful;*
> *If a teaching shows God to be all-powerful,*
> *… not dependent upon man for anything;*
> *If a teaching humbles man,*
> *… showing him to be needful of God in all things*
> *… and the servant of his fellow men;*
> *The teaching is true.*

⋞ও৶ঌ

> *If a teaching takes glory from God,*
> *… making him appear unloving, unjust, or unmerciful;*
> *If a teaching limits God's power to act*
> *… until man has accomplished something;*
> *If a teaching puffs man up,*
> *… setting man equal to God*
> *… or giving him or his group power over others;*
> *The teaching is false.*

Teachings and interpretations that fail to pass this test, no matter how firmly established as Christian doctrine, should be reexamined and reconsidered: if we refuse to do so we, too, will be guilty of ignoring the Will of God for the sake of our traditions.

⋞ও৶ঌ

Examined through the *Sieve of the Spokesmen*, there are two doctrines central to Christianity that have the handprints of Man all over them:

- Belief in Jesus is required for salvation;
- Christians should make disciples of all the nations. (The "Great Commission")

Combined, these doctrines make it incumbent upon Christians to convert non-believers and believers in other religions to Christianity; otherwise they will spend eternity in Hell. ... This has become the bedrock of institutionalized Christianity, the firm foundation upon which the Church itself is built. It thus seems blasphemous to suggest that this is *not* what Jesus taught, that it runs *counter* to what Jesus taught, and that it has contributed to the world's failure to embrace Christianity. These are serious charges, and I do not make them lightly. Let me outline for you the evidence that leads to these conclusions.

First, the teachings clearly fail to pass the *Sieve of the Spokesmen* test: they take power away from God by limiting God's power to act – to save – until Man has succeeded in converting someone. In effect they teach that no matter how good and loving a person is, unless that person assents to belief in Christ there is nothing God can do to save him: instead, Man alone has the power to save by converting him. Thus the teachings affirm our instinctive belief that our tribe is superior, and justify, even make noble, our instinct to impose our beliefs on others. It is because these teachings are so naturally resonant with our tribal nature that they have become deep-rooted in Christianity. ... Realizing that the teachings align with our tribal nature rather than our spiritual nature, however, should make Christians pause and weigh these teachings against Jesus' other teachings.

A second reason for Christians to pause is to consider the harm inflicted by blindly following these doctrines. If when we came to believe in Jesus as the Son of God we instantly became all-knowing and understanding of "the Way" there would be no problem. But, as Paul taught, that is not the case: we first are "babes in Christ" who must be nurtured to continually grow in Christ, to increasingly overcome our tribal nature. It is a matter of historical record that too often Christians, inflated by their power, have set out as still flawed representatives of Christ to convert others, and their flaws have turned away those they are trying to convert. Is it any wonder that potential converts exposed to seductive or manipulative "Christians" would reject believing in their God? But our doctrines allow no quarter: if anyone rejects Christ, no matter how justified the reasons, they are doomed to eternal hellfire. This, too, violates the *Sieve of the Spokesmen* for it makes God appear unloving, unjust, and unmerciful.

Similarly, these doctrines allow no empathy or concern for the family relationships of the converts. When a loved member of a family converts to another religion, it causes great anguish and distress within the family, perhaps even destroying it. That can be of no concern, however, for the importance of saving a soul requires accepting whatever "collateral damage" is inflicted on non-believers. (After all, they're non-people, not of our tribe.) This callous, unloving indifference to the feelings of others is justified only if the stakes are as high as we believe them to be: that unless a person, good or bad, comes to believe in Christ they are irrevocably doomed to eternal damnation. ...

But what if that is not true?

What if that is a "teaching of Men" rather than of Jesus?

In Chapter 9, *Gospels vs. Gospels*, we examined the Gospel verses addressing whether or not belief in Jesus is required for salvation. We found that, yes, there are many verses justifying this doctrine, but we also found there are significant other verses challenging it:

> I tell you the truth, **all the sins and blasphemies of men will be forgiven them**. But **whoever blasphemes against the Holy Spirit will never be forgiven**; he is guilty of an eternal sin. (Mark 3:28-29)

*And so I tell you, every sin and blasphemy will be forgiven men, but the blasphemy against the Spirit will not be forgiven. **Anyone who speaks a word against the Son of Man will be forgiven, but anyone who speaks against the Holy Spirit will not be forgiven**, either in this age or in the age to come.*
(Matt 12:31-32)

*… **everyone who speaks a word against the Son of Man will be forgiven, but anyone who blasphemes against the Holy Spirit will not be forgiven**.*
(Luke 12:10)

*… **if anyone hears my words and does not observe them, I do not condemn him**, for I did not come to condemn the world but to save the world.*
(John 12:47)

If Jesus specifically taught that even those who blasphemed against him would be forgiven, not condemned, how can it possibly be true that those who simply didn't believe in him would be condemned?

We also looked at Jesus' parable of the sheep and the goats:

"When the Son of Man comes in his glory, and all the angels with him, he will sit upon his glorious throne, and all the nations will be assembled before him. And he will separate them one from another, as a shepherd separates the sheep from the goats. He will place the sheep on his right and the goats on his left. Then the king will say to those on his right, 'Come, you who are blessed by my Father. Inherit the kingdom prepared for you from the foundation of the world. For I was hungry and you gave me food, I was thirsty and you gave me drink, a stranger and you welcomed me, naked and you clothed me, ill and you cared for me, in prison and you visited me.' Then the righteous will answer him and say, 'Lord, when did we see you hungry and feed you, or thirsty and give you drink? When did we see you a stranger and welcome you, or naked and clothe you? When did we see you ill or in prison, and visit you?' And the king will say to them in reply, 'Amen, I say to you, whatever you did for one of these least brothers of mine, you did for me.' Then he will say to those on his left, 'Depart from me, you accursed, into the eternal fire prepared for the devil and his angels. For I was hungry and you gave me no food, I was thirsty and you gave me no drink, a stranger and you gave me no welcome, naked and you gave me

no clothing, ill and in prison, and you did not care for me.' Then they will answer and say, 'Lord, when did we see you hungry or thirsty or a stranger or naked or ill or in prison, and not minister to your needs?' He will answer them, 'Amen, I say to you, what you did not do for one of these least ones, you did not do for me. 'And these will go off to eternal punishment, but the righteous to eternal life."
(Matt 25:31-46)

In this powerful parable, the "Saved" were not saved because of a professed belief in the Son of Man, but specifically because they cared for their fellowman. … And in another parable, one that should strike, if not fear, at least concern in the hearts of professed believers, Jesus taught:

"Not everyone who says to me, 'Lord, Lord,' will enter the kingdom of heaven, but only the one who does the will of my Father in heaven. Many will say to me on that day, 'Lord, Lord, did we not prophesy in your name? Did we not drive out demons in your name? Did we not do mighty deeds in your name?' Then I will declare to them solemnly, 'I never knew you. Depart from me, you evildoers.'
(Matt 7:21-23)

Here, people who not only believed in Jesus but did works in his name were nonetheless rejected! This is incomprehensible unless seen as an example of Jesus' teaching that it's our inner motivations that are important rather than our outer actions. … Serving Christ for expected reward rather than love of fellowmen is insufficient, and we can only assume that this was the reason for their rejection.

Jesus' Parable of the Good Samaritan, also taught that caring for one's neighbor was more important than professed beliefs, for the Jews and Samaritans had strongly differing beliefs.

… "A man fell victim to robbers as he went down from Jerusalem to Jericho. They stripped and beat him and went off leaving him half-dead. A priest happened to be going down that road, but when he saw him, he passed by on the opposite side. Likewise a Levite came to the place, and when he saw him, he passed by on the opposite side. But a Samaritan traveler who came upon him was moved with compassion at the sight. He approached the victim, poured oil and wine over his wounds and bandaged

them. ... Which of these three, in your opinion, was neighbor to the man who fell in with the robbers? The answer came, "The one who treated him with compassion." Jesus said, "Then go and do the same."
(Luke 10:30-34, 36-37)

Despite these significant teachings challenging the doctrine that belief in Jesus is required for salvation, Christianity has continually ignored them in favor of the teachings that indulge our self-serving tribal nature. While Jesus taught that we should be the servants of our fellowman ...

"You know that the rulers of the Gentiles lord it over them, and the great ones make their authority over them felt. But it shall not be so among you. Rather, whoever wishes to be great among you shall be your servant; whoever wishes to be first among you shall be your slave. Just so, the Son of Man did not come to be served but to serve and to give his life as a ransom for many."
(Matt 20:25-28)

... we prefer teachings that effectively make us masters over them: no matter if they may be more loving and caring of their fellowman than we ourselves, they are nonetheless doomed to the everlasting fires of Hades unless we intervene and save them ... or so we believe, in spite of the teachings of Jesus that suggest otherwise.

❦

If we accept that loving our neighbors as ourselves is equivalent to loving God, and that is all that is necessary to be saved, how then should we understand the "Great Commission" of Matthew 28:16-20?

The eleven disciples went to Galilee, to the mountain to which Jesus had ordered them. When they saw him, they worshiped, but they doubted. Then Jesus approached and said to them, "All power in heaven and on earth has been given to me. Go, therefore, and make disciples of all nations, baptizing them in the name of the Father, and of the Son, and of the holy Spirit, teaching them to observe all that I have commanded you. And behold, I am with you always, until the end of the age."

Were it true that professing a belief in Jesus is necessary to be saved, even if the proselytizing is done by seducing or manipulating flawed Christians, then the command to "make" disciples of the nations would be comprehensible and clearly necessary. But if it is recognized that professing a belief in Jesus is *not* a requirement for salvation, then the Great Commission can be seen as being potentially harmful: rather than being witnesses for Christ wherever we are, spreading his teachings and demonstrating them with our love for one another, the commission can seduce us into the tribally satisfying zeal of imposing our beliefs on others and seeing ourselves – rather than God – as their "saviors."

When we look for Scripture to support Matthew's Great Commission, we are surprised to find there isn't any. Just as the Gospels' birth narratives differ significantly in detail, so do the Gospels' narratives of Jesus' last words to his followers: where Matthew describes them as occurring in Galilee, as quoted above, Mark describes them as occurring in Jerusalem;

> *He said to them, "Go into the whole world and proclaim the gospel to every creature.*
> (Mark 16:15)

Luke describes them as occurring at Bethany;

> *And he said to them, "Thus it is written that the Messiah would suffer and rise from the dead on the third day and that repentance, for the forgiveness of sins, would be preached in his name to all the nations, beginning from Jerusalem.*
> (Luke 24:46-47)

John describes them as occurring in Jerusalem;

> *(Jesus) said to them again, "Peace be with you. As the Father has sent me, so I send you." And when he had said this, he breathed on them and said to them, "Receive the holy Spirit. Whose sins you forgive are forgiven them, and whose sins you retain are retained."*
> (John 20:21-23)

and Acts describes them as occurring at Mt. Olive;

> *He answered them, "It is not for you to know the times or seasons that the Father has established by his own authority. But you will receive power when the holy Spirit comes upon you, and you will be my witnesses in Jerusalem, throughout Judea and Samaria, and to the ends of the earth. When he had said this, as they were looking on, he was lifted up, and a cloud took him from their sight."*
> (Acts 1:7-9)

Note the wordings used by the writers other than Mathew:

> *... Go into the whole world and proclaim the gospel to every creature;* (Mark)

> *... repentance for the forgiveness of sins would be preached in his name to all the nations;* (Luke)

> *... As the Father has sent me, so I send you ... Whose sins you forgive are forgiven them, and whose sins you retain are retained;* (John)

> *... you will be my witnesses in Jerusalem, throughout Judea and Samaria, and to the ends of the earth.* (Acts)

The wordings show Jesus telling his disciples to proclaim the Gospel throughout the world ... but *not* commanding them to "make disciples of the nations." Of all the descriptions of Jesus' parting words, only the single verse in Matthew contains the command to *make* disciples. ... Shouldn't so important a command be attested to elsewhere, even throughout Jesus' teachings?

Searching for corroboration in the other recorded teachings of Jesus, however, discloses not only that there is none, but that the command itself is out of character for Jesus. In none of Jesus' teachings did he ever instruct someone to tell another person what to do. Instead, he inevitably told those seeking his support to address themselves, their own attitudes and actions – the "log in their own eye" – rather than those of someone else. Even when he sent out the Twelve and Seventy-Two to the towns of Galilee, he instructed them only to heal and to preach the Kingdom of God, not to "make" disciples.

Nonetheless, despite the teaching being out of character for Jesus and having no support elsewhere in the Gospels, our tribal urge to impose our beliefs on others is so compelling that we have made it a central tenet of Christianity, a tenet that has been responsible for much of the criticism of institutionalized Christianity over the centuries: our zeal for making converts has too often overshadowed our zeal for spreading Jesus' message wherever we are, and demonstrating it with our love for one another.

⊱⊰

There are other teachings of Jesus that Christianity has persistently ignored in favor of preferred teachings. In Chapter 9, *Gospels vs. Gospels*, we examined Gospel verses that continued the Hebrew Bible/Old Testament debate over whether God does or does not intervene to reward the Good and punish the Evil on Earth. We found that there are many verses justifying a "health and wealth" doctrine, that following Jesus will result in earthly reward. For example ...

> *Give and gifts will be given to you; a good measure, packed together, shaken down, and overflowing, will be poured into your lap. For the measure with which you measure will in return be measured out to you.*
> (Luke 6:38)

But we also found there are significant contrasting verses calling upon Jesus' followers to "take up their cross," to disregard material possessions, and to expect suffering and persecution rather than reward as a result of following him. For example ...

> *He summoned the crowd with his disciples and said to them, "Whoever wishes to come after me must deny himself, take up his cross, and follow me. For whoever wishes to save his life will lose it, but whoever loses his life for my sake and that of the gospel will save it.*
> (Mark 8:34-35)

To reconcile the contrasts, we wondered if when Jesus promised earthly rewards he was speaking of earthly *spiritual* rewards rather than earthly *material* rewards. For example ...

Instead, seek his kingdom, and these other things will be given you besides. ... Sell your belongings and give alms. Provide money bags for yourselves that do not wear out, an inexhaustible treasure in heaven that no thief can reach nor moth destroy. For where your treasure is, there also will your heart be.
(Luke 12:31-34)

Then finally we noted that there are verses where Jesus taught plainly that God not only did not intervene to reward the Good and punish the Bad, but that God treated the Good and Bad alike and that we should do the same!

*But rather, love your enemies and do good to them, and lend expecting nothing back; then your reward will be great and you will be children of the Most High, **for he himself is kind to the ungrateful and the wicked**. Be merciful, just as (also) your Father is merciful*
(Luke 6:35-36)

*But I say to you, love your enemies, and pray for those who persecute you, that you may be children of your heavenly Father, **for he makes his sun rise on the bad and the good, and causes rain to fall on the just and the unjust**.*
(Matthew 5:44-45)

*At that time some people who were present there told him about the Galileans whose blood Pilate had mingled with the blood of their sacrifices. He said to them in reply, **"Do you think that because these Galileans suffered in this way they were greater sinners than all other Galileans?** By no means! But I tell you, if you do not repent, you will all perish as they did! Or those eighteen people who were killed when the tower at Siloam fell on them—**do you think they were more guilty than everyone else who lived in Jerusalem?** By no means! But I tell you, if you do not repent, you will all perish as they did!"*
(Luke 13:1-5)

The conflict between what we want – divine justice in our favor – and what we observe,

... there are just men treated as though they had done evil and wicked men treated as though they had done justly.
(Eccl 8:14)

... runs throughout the Hebrew Bible/Old Testament and the New Testament. Our very (human) nature screams out against what we see as injustice, and we rage to make it right. ... But we need to repeatedly remind ourselves that we are flawed judges: we see everything through our tribal biases and, given the opportunity, we are certain – in the name of Justice – to impose injustices that favor us. ... Hence, Jesus' teachings to judge not, and to forgive our enemies.

⚞⚟

A final question to consider is what Jesus taught and did not teach on "social justice." In Chapter 12, *Jesus as Reform Prophet*, we reviewed the teachings of Jesus and saw that they echoed and amplified the Reform Prophets' teachings, but there was one surprising exception: where the Reform Prophets railed against the rulers of Israel and Judah for oppressing the poor and needy ...

> Then I said, "Listen, you leaders of Jacob, you rulers of the house of Israel. Should you not know justice, you who hate good and love evil; who tear the skin from my people and the flesh from their bones?"
> (Micah 3:1-2)

... Jesus spoke only against *religious* leaders (the Priests, Scribes and Pharisees), and called for *religious* reform rather than *social* reform. Rather than demanding social justice for all, Jesus instead taught how we as individuals should respond when we experience injustice: inevitably he called upon us to reexamine our own position, our own inner attitudes.

Of course Jesus was opposed to injustice!

But the injustices of the world are *symptoms* of the underlying disease, and Jesus spoke against the disease itself: the corruption of Religion by religious leaders to serve Man rather than serving God and improving Man. There will be no end to the rampant injustice in this world – now or ever – until and unless Christianity weeds out the self-serving teachings of Men and becomes a credible witness for Christ to the world.

⚞⚟

Is this possible? ... Is it possible that a Christianity which has historically preferred quarreling over doctrines rather than "becoming one" ever going to be able to do that?

Astonishingly, it is not only possible, but possible with only a small change in our understanding of our doctrines, and in a way that will allow Christian tribes to coexist and work together for the good of Mankind. The next and final chapter, *What Christianity Should Teach*, describes that way.

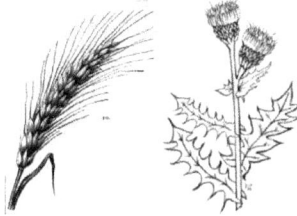

Chapter 14.
What Christianity Should Teach

First, a summary of what has brought us here …

Even though we, Mankind, have always formed tribes and warred with one another, we have steadfastly rejected the possibility that we did so because we were tribal territorial animals motivated by instincts. We rejected this possibility because, first, we couldn't detect any instincts influencing our behavior, and, second, we always had "rational" reasons for our warring.

Both of these objections have been overcome by the last half century of brain research: it has been demonstrated repeatedly and irrefutably that our brain contains an "interpreter" function that generates strongly believed "rational" explanations for anything we feel or do in response to subconscious motivations. … This function effectively masks our instincts, enabling us to be tribal territorial animals programmed to war and quarrel with one another, yet to be totally unaware of the instincts provoking our consistently irrational behavior.

This does *not* mean that our behavior is *predestined*, however, only that it is *predisposed* by our instincts. We, unique among animals, have the capacity to override our instincts and have done so throughout our existence, primarily through religious and secular cultural teachings … "Wisdom" teachings.

The continuous struggle between *"the Spirit"* and *"the Flesh"* portrayed in Scripture, particularly the New Testament, is more than an analogy: it is a reality, a description of the continual battle between our instincts and the sheath of cultural beliefs we develop to constrain them. God, as the *Spirit of Goodness*, the *Holy Spirit*, has provided us with an internal desire for justice and mercy which motivates us to be good … to be better … to work towards overcoming our animal instinct to dominate or destroy other tribes.

Our tribal programming is so powerful, however, that throughout our existence we have rarely, if ever, been able to overcome our compulsion to war with one another. The entire history of Man is a history of warring empires, and we are in very real danger of eventually destroying ourselves in our quest to destroy others.

The teachings of Jesus directly oppose our harmful tribal instincts: the teachings of Jesus instruct us, dramatically, to remove the log from our own eye … to go the second mile … to repay evil with good … to love our enemies. If followed, they provide a desperately needed antidote to our destructive behavior.

Dismayingly, rather than applying Jesus' teaching – even in our relationships with other Christians – we have instead succumbed to our tribal impulses to treat those with differing Christian doctrines as enemies and to fight with them for dominance … a wanton betrayal of Christ's teachings and a false witness to the world.

The time has come for redemption.

The time has come for Christian religious leaders, clergy and lay alike, to accept Christ's chastisement and recognize that *they* (*we*) have become the ones standing in the way and placing burdens – teachings of Men – upon others. Our denominational and non-denominational tribes are like clay idols that instead of being decorated with bits of colored glass are decorated with "doctrines" and "sacraments," each having its own unique outward appearance and its own unique collection of dogma. Beneath their mud-daubed surfaces, however, glows the eternal

Spirit of Goodness, and the Spirit's message shines through the cracks as the "good" teachings within our religions. Those teachings together form an overlay, an outline of our instinctive image of God and Goodness, and provide a template for what "perfect" Man should be. If ever Man is to be "saved" from himself, it will have to be through these teachings, elevated to the world-wide religion of a single tribe, Mankind, and a single race, the Human race.

This is miraculous! ... Although we are incapable of negotiating our beliefs with others, we are nonetheless capable of bypassing them entirely with a larger, more encompassing truth or belief!

We can't give up our doctrines – they are what define us – but we *can* give up claiming they are of importance to God and must be believed to be saved. ... We can instead teach that while we think our particular doctrines are worthy vehicles for understanding and serving God, it is caring for our fellowman that is of ultimate importance, and all who do so are "children of God." ... We can maintain our fealty to our tribal doctrines, but cease imposing them on others and instead witness that all who love are of God, and that Jesus' teachings show the way. ... Our denominations and non-denominations can retain their unique practices, symbols, and rituals, their seminaries, publishing houses, and retirement plans, but must give up any insistence that their teachings provide the only way to salvation, and any reluctance to treat other brothers and sisters in Christ as equals.

Thus it *is* possible – and vitally necessary – for Christianity to reform itself and "become one, that the world might believe." ... It is vitally necessary for Christianity to show the world, through its zeal and service to its fellowmen, that the teachings of Jesus really do provide the means of saving Mankind ... from itself.

The remainder of this chapter – and this book – recommends what Christianity *should* teach on the major issues defining Christianity. Christianity has an incredibly rich history, and no single Christian's understanding can possibly encompass its many facets. My recommendations reflect my personal three-score-ten-years labor to understand Scripture and be a better servant of Christ. When you find yourself disagreeing – perhaps vehemently – remind yourself that *all* of our preferred interpretations, teachings, and doctrines, both yours and mine, are of importance only to us and not to God, who cares only that we demonstrate our love for Him by loving our fellowman, and treating them as we want to be treated. … Our many differing doctrines are tolerable only so long as we do not try to impose them upon others, for if we do, we are joining the ranks of the religious leaders Jesus criticized for placing burdens upon others and standing in their way. To avoid this, Christianity should evaluate *all* of its teachings with the *Sieve of the Spokesmen*:

> *If a teaching gives glory to God,*
> *… showing him to be loving, just, and merciful;*
> *If a teaching shows God to be all-powerful,*
> *… not dependent upon man for anything;*
> *If a teaching humbles man,*
> *… showing him to be needful of God in all things*
> *… and the servant of his fellow men;*
> *The teaching is true.*

⤜⤛

> *If a teaching takes glory from God,*
> *… making him appear unloving, unjust, or unmerciful;*
> *If a teaching limits God's power to act*
> *… until man has accomplished something;*
> *If a teaching puffs man up,*
> *… setting man equal to God*
> *… or giving him or his group power over others;*
> *The teaching is false.*

Here, then, are sample recommendations of what Christianity *should* teach, given our growing understanding of the nature of Man and the nature of God.

On the Trinity

Surprisingly, the Holy Trinity is *not* the mystery theologians have portrayed it to be: it is simply a reflection of the three ways we experience God: we experience God as the Creator and Master of the Universe and "all that dwell therein"; we experience God in the being and works of Jesus on earth; and we experience God through the prompting and urgings of the Holy Spirit, "God Within Us," the "Spirit of Goodness."

Unfortunately, it is Man's tendency to convert common sense observations into formal doctrines and dogma, and then have to spin off even more doctrines and dogma to explain the shortcomings and oversights in the first. ... Thus the many volumes explaining the "mystery" of the Trinity.

On the Nature of God

We experience God as the Creator and Master of the Universe and "all that dwell therein."

God, the Creator of the Universe and "all that dwell therein," is transcendent, alive, and permeates every particle of Creation, particularly Man. While the mind of Man cannot comprehend the mind of God ...

Will what is made say to its maker, "Why have you created me so?" (Romans 9:20)

... we nonetheless were created, not so much "*in the image of God,*" but with the image of God implanted within us. "*The Holy Spirit*" ... "*God Within Us*" ... goads us to overcome our animal impulses to war with others and harm those not of our tribe: this contention between "*the Spirit*" and "*the Flesh*" is intrinsic, elemental, and ongoing: it will endure to the End Times.

In spite of the presence of *God Within Us*, throughout our existence we have maligned and tarnished the image of God with self-serving distortions attempting to justify our instinct to dominate and destroy our enemies: from our portraying Him as a self-indulgent potentate who created us to enjoy our praise and sweet-smelling burnt offerings, to a malignant warlord who ordered our genocidal attacks on others, to an arbitrary, rubber-stamping bureaucrat who will punish all who do not bow to our dogma and doctrines.

Because of such self-serving misrepresentations of God, it is sometimes claimed that "Man created God in Man's image," and Scripture indeed documents that Man has attempted to do this ... with animal-headed gods and goddesses endorsing our lust for power, and fertility gods and goddesses endorsing our lust for good harvests ... and for lust. But the God of Judeo-Christianity, far from reflecting an image of earthly Man, projects an image of what heavenly Man, perfected Man, should be.

Consider, can any living creature envision God in any way other than as a perfect example of its own species, an example to be strived for and emulated?

So be perfect, just as your heavenly Father is perfect.
(Matt 5:48)

Were we seagulls we could only conceive of God as the perfect seagull, and were we wolves we could only conceive of God as the perfect wolf; as humans we can only conceive of God as the perfect Man/Woman, the perfect example of how we should live and behave throughout our life. ... Thus we conceive of God as a loving Father/Mother who knows His/Her children and guides and instructs them how to handle the challenges of life; the instruction provides us the strength to be faithful and caring of others in all circumstances, and teaches that while giving in to temptations to be dominating and hedonistic may bring short-term pleasure, it ultimately brings death.

The major monotheistic religions, Judaism, Christianity, and Islam, all teach that *The One God* created the heavens, the earth, and all the peoples on earth. ... They also teach that their founders and followers are particularly favored by *The One God* over all the others – reminding us of Mark Twain's quote that, *"Man ... is the only animal that has the True Religion – several of them."* The other, "not-major" religions, whether monotheistic, polytheistic, or non-theistic, similarly portray their god(s) and God-equivalents as favoring them and their true beliefs over others. ... Given this documented and observable reality, what should Christianity teach about God's relationship with *all* the peoples of the earth that He created?

Chapter 2, *From the Beginning,* hypothesized that the world's religions arose as the result of our brain's interpreter function generating explanations for our tribal feelings and behaviors:

> *"No matter where on Earth our early forebears arose, their teachings codified and justified our instinctive tribal behavior: the teachings reflected both our good side – to be caring and self-sacrificing for tribemates – and our bad – to dominate or destroy rival tribes."*

The teachings were cloaked in differing cultural guises, but all reflected our internal God-given instincts: our teachings on the Holy Spirit, for example, arose from the *God-within-us* instinct to be Good. As a consequence, it should be expected that all the resultant religions would have both "good" teachings, to be caring of others, and "bad" teachings, to dominate others. Most religions, for example, have some form of the "Golden Rule," and most teach that only those sharing their sacred beliefs are acceptable to God.

Christianity should acknowledge this reality, and lead the way in reforming religion by emphasizing the good teachings and deemphasizing the bad. ... If there is only one God, there can be only one "true faith," and that is the faith that is fully in accord with God's will for Man. This "true faith" is the measure of all religions, including Christianity: a religion is "true" insofar as it is in accord with the true faith – God's will for Man – and is "false" insofar as it is not.

Christianity should willingly and openly invite comparing its understanding of God's will for Man, based on the teachings of Jesus, with those of other religions and should encourage that the "*Sieve of the Spokesmen*" be applied to all. ... Are Christians not to be the servant of their fellowmen rather than their master?

On the Nature of Jesus
We experience God in the being and works of Jesus.

Jesus is truly the Son of God in the only way that matters: he did the will of his Father. Why do we presume that for Jesus to be the Son of God his conception had to be miraculous, as if God could not instill His Spirit into one naturally conceived?

It is historically observable that whenever humans want to demonstrate the divinity of a person they present a narrative of that person being miraculously conceived: we do this so consistently that it's apparently a predisposition, a part of our nature. Acknowledging this, however, tells us nothing about whether Jesus was or was not divinely conceived ... only that both are possibilities. Maintaining either position (or any other speculation about the nature of Jesus' divinity) as a belief does no harm as long as believing it is not imposed as a requirement for salvation.

Recognizing, however, that God could instill His Spirit into Jesus with or without a miraculous conception removes the need to *insist* on a miraculous conception, and allows teaching instead that Jesus is truly the Son of God in the only way that matters – he did the will of his Father – and that we should follow his teachings and strive, too, to be children of God in the only way that matters, by obeying His Will to love one another.

The utter, bedrock insight and belief of Christianity is that God allowed His beloved Son Jesus to die as a sacrifice for the sins of Mankind; we are saved by the shedding of Jesus' blood, and we should joyously follow in His footsteps and teachings by loving and serving our fellowman.

Beyond this essential truth, however, Christianity (being human) has continuously speculated over the many scripturally ambiguous or unspecified details of Jesus' ministry: did Jesus really die for the sins of *all* Mankind? ... to what degree was Jesus aware of his divinity? ... at what point in his ministry (and post-resurrection appearances) did his followers realize he was the Son of God and not just the Jewish Messiah?

To fill in the ambiguous or unspecified details, Christianity has formulated doctrines – teachings of Men – but these doctrines often raise even more questions: for example, the doctrine that only those who believe in Jesus as the Son of God are saved effectively teaches that Jesus did *not* die for the sins of all Mankind but only for the sins of those who believe in him. ... Similarly, doctrines speculating to what degree Jesus was aware of his divinity, or at what point his followers realized he was the Son of God and not just the Jewish Messiah, provided more opportunities for Christians to divide, clash, and be dismissed as a viperous mass of quarrelsome sects.

Christianity should acknowledge and accept that the Gospels and Epistles do *not* provide unequivocal answers to the many questions we raise, and that while we would *like* answers to these questions they are not essential to the Christian message: it can be believed (at one extreme) that Jesus was aware of his divine mission from conception and that his disciples were fully aware of it by the time of his post-resurrection appearances; or it can be believed (at another extreme) that Jesus became aware of his role only gradually – through the Holy Spirit and study of Scripture – and that his followers became aware of it only after his post-resurrection appearance to Paul and Paul's subsequent preaching. Neither of these (nor any other) speculative interpretations of the nature of Jesus being "truly God and truly Man" alter the essential Truth ...

God allowed His beloved Son Jesus to die as a sacrifice for the sins of Mankind; we are saved by the shedding of Jesus' blood, and we should joyously follow in His footsteps and teachings by loving and serving our fellowman.

On the Nature of the Holy Spirit

We experience God through the prompting and urgings of the Holy Spirit, "God Within Us," the "Spirit of Goodness."

The Holy Spirit, "God Within Us," provides the means and motivation to recognize and honor God's "works and ways" in the world and in our lives: it is through the Spirit that we recognize God's work in Creation and in Jesus; it is through the Spirit that we recognize God's presence and activity in our lives; it is through the Spirit that we pray and converse with God/Jesus; it is the Spirit that provides us words to speak as witnesses; it is the Spirit that intercedes for us when we groan, brokenly, inarticulately, for help; "the Spirit scrutinizes everything, even the depths of God."

This understanding of the Holy Spirit's intimate relationship with us comes through the New Testament. While both the Old and the New Testaments testify that the Holy Spirit has always been with Man ... being present at Creation and speaking through David and the Prophets ... in the Old Testament the Spirit appears mostly as an external force, *"the Spirit of the Lord,"* that periodically *"comes upon"* Men to motivate them to action, but demonstrating little empathy or intimacy with them.

In contrast, the New Testament describes the Holy Spirit as dwelling within us, interacting with us, and having great empathy for our earthly trials and tribulations. This dramatic change in the Holy Spirit (or of Man's understanding of the Holy Spirit) is reflected in the Gospel of John's account that Jesus, prior to his ascension, promised his followers that he would send them a "Comforter," an "Advocate," "the Spirit of Truth" to be with them. Thereafter in the New Testament (particularly in Acts and the Epistles) the Holy Spirit is portrayed as having the intimate relationship with Man ascribed to "the Comforter," and as only being present in those who believed in and followed Jesus ... those who were baptized in the name of Jesus and had hands laid upon them.

The New Testament does not provide an explanation of the changing, sometimes differing, sometimes overlapping descriptions and roles of the Holy Spirit, Comforter, Advocate, or Spirit of Truth. All, however, show God dwelling with and within us, and providing a constant, ongoing, intimate relationship which is our refuge and our strength, our help in time of trouble.

Christianity must accept, acknowledge, and constantly remind itself that the New Testament was not written as a closed theological document but rather to persuade, encourage, and comfort new believers in Christ. Attempts to distill and impose particular doctrines from its many, varied witness accounts and teachings are misguided, divisive, and directly oppose Christ's injunction "to be one," to be one in the Spirit, to be one in the Lord.

On the Nature of Satan

Does "Satan" exist? ...

Psychologically and empirically, "Yes!"

The pioneering psychiatrist and psychoanalyst Carl G. Jung (1875-1961) developed the concept of Man having a "collective unconscious," a common body of instinctive knowledge that contained templates, or "archetypes," for all the creatures and circumstances likely to be encountered from infancy through old age: he postulated that the templates become operative when a real-life pattern matching them is encountered, and provide a framework for interpreting and evaluating persons and events. Archetypes for Mother, Father, God, Satan, Demons, Heroes, Wise Old Men/Women, etc., were described.

He based his theory on the documented evidence that human societies throughout history and around the world have developed remarkably similar stories ("myths") about these commonly experienced characters and circumstances. Had knowledge of DNA encoding and computer programming existed earlier, it is very likely Jung would have postulated instead "collective *programming*" containing "*subprograms*" that predispose us to particular behavior in particular circumstances. Jung's archetypes can now be seen as conscious personifications generated in response to Man's unconscious instincts.

Some concept of "Satan" – the Devil in any of his guises – is universal throughout human societies, and is consequently one of the archetypes postulated by Jung. Psychologically, as the personification of the evil latent within us, Satan *does* exist, and this personification is not only "real" to us, it is essential to our efforts to not succumb to urges for evil. Rather than attempting to resist harmful temptations with reason alone – which is foolhardy and prone to fail – it is far better to invoke the naturally occurring personification "Satan" to summon up innate defensive programs to aid us: by seeing evil impulses as the work of an Enemy wanting to destroy us, we trigger the powerful emotions accompanying fighting off an enemy and enlist them to fight our urges. … When we're told, for example,

> Your opponent the devil is prowling around like a roaring lion looking for (someone) to devour …
> (1 Peter 5:8)

our defensive mechanisms become aroused and alert to defend us from possible attack. (That the Devil is ever prowling and we're never safe from him is a particularly apt metaphor, since he dwells within us as the advocate of our evil impulses, is ever present, and is indeed our enemy.)

Secularists, however, believe Man is wholly rational and not subject to instincts as are all other animals: as a consequence whenever Scripture employs language or examples reflecting Man's intrinsic nature (prewired with moral judgements and personifications) they reflexively dismiss it as "superstition."

Christianity should instruct secularists that the Modern Evolutionary Synthesis (which they claim to believe) *requires* that humans have instincts: within Evolutionary theory there is no

> ... "A*nd then a miracle occurred, and Man was freed from the bonds of instinct.*"

Scripture accurately reflects the influence of Man's instincts on Man's behavior, and is a far better explanator of human behavior than the secularist theories blindly denying their existence.

On Original Sin

From the second century C.E. onward, theologians have entertained every conceivable doctrinal position on whether Adam and Eve's sin of eating the forbidden fruit in the Garden of Eden affected their offspring – Us – and whether we are consequently born innocent or guilty of sin. All of the resulting doctrines are teachings of Men, not of God. ... Rather than speculating about "Original Sin," Christianity should teach on Man's "original flaw," which is ongoing and potentially fatal: wanting to be equal to God and free from Godly restraints.

Throughout history Man has repeatedly tried to escape the God-given cultural restraints protecting him from himself, and has repeatedly suffered the collapse of his society as a result. The Hebrew Bible/Old Testament warns Man of such hubris in the accounts of eating the forbidden fruit and building the Tower of Babel, but Man sadly persists in trying to replace God with Reason, and in rationalizing excuses for self-destructive hedonistic behavior.

On the Means of Salvation

Christianity should teach, as did Jesus and the Reform Prophets, that all are saved who believe in (and practice) treating others as they themselves would want to be treated. Did not Jesus teach us ...

> Not everyone who says to me, 'Lord, Lord,' will enter the kingdom of heaven, but only the one who does the will of my Father in heaven. (Matt 7:21)

... and if we substitute "gospel" for "law" in Paul's letter to the Romans it teaches us ...

> For it is not those who hear the gospel who are righteous in God's sight, but it is those who do his will who will be declared righteous. Indeed, when non-believers, who do not have the gospel, do by nature things required by the gospel, they are a gospel for themselves, even though they do not have the gospel, since they show that the requirements of the gospel are written on their hearts ... (Romans 2:13-15a, modified)

Our awareness of an obligation to be Good comes through the Spirit, and believing in that obligation is believing in its Source – even if unknowingly – just as loving our neighbor is loving God, even if unknowingly.

The only "unforgivable sin," the only sin that prevents salvation, is denying the God-given Spirit that makes us aware of God's word written (through instincts) on our hearts.

On Death, Resurrection, and Judgement

Chapter 9, *Gospels vs. Gospels*, described Scripture's interwoven strands of Judeo and Greco-Roman beliefs on death and resurrection. Over time they evolved from a belief that death was a descent into Sheol – from which there was no return – to a belief that Man has a mortal body and an immortal soul, and at death the body perishes but the soul ascends – perhaps for reward or punishment as deserved.

By Jesus' time, there was a clear division between those who believed there would be a resurrection of the dead (notably the Pharisees, Jesus, and his followers) and those who retained the traditional belief that there would be no resurrection (notably the Sadducees.)

The majority of Christianity today – as evidenced by our funeral sermons and services – believe that we have immortal souls that leave our bodies at death and are either united with God and Jesus in Heaven or banished to Hades with Satan, both for all eternity. ... Jesus described such a scenario in his Parable of the Last Judgement:

> Then he will say to those on his left, 'Depart from me, you accursed, into the eternal fire prepared for the devil and his angels. ... And these will go off to eternal punishment, but the righteous to eternal life."
> (Matt 25:41-46)

But we also believe – as evidenced by our various creeds and doctrines – that there will be a resurrection of the body in some form at the End Times. There is no generally accepted doctrine reconciling these two prevailing beliefs: immediate judgement and deliverance to Heaven or Hell at death, or resurrection and judgement delayed until the End Times. But just as the two conflicting birth narratives in Matthew and Luke do not bother us, neither do these two conflicting death narratives. As with the nature of Jesus, maintaining a preferred viewpoint causes no harm as long as it is not imposed as a requirement for salvation.

Christianity should recognize and teach that in all such circumstances, whenever Scripture doesn't present a single, consistent, indisputable description of an event or concept, no doctrine should be imposed since differing doctrines can be derived depending upon which verses are selected and emphasized. While we can *recommend* our preferred doctrines, we must at the same time acknowledge that loving our fellowman is more important than loving our doctrines, and trying to impose our doctrines on our fellowman is not loving.

On Heaven, and Hell

It appears that throughout Scripture Man has envisioned Heaven as an extrapolation of all the treasures, pleasures, and happiness's of earth magnified many fold ...

> He will wipe every tear from their eyes, and there shall be no more death or mourning, wailing or pain, (for) the old order has passed away."
> (Rev 21:4)

> He ... showed me the holy city Jerusalem coming down out of heaven from God. ... Its radiance was like that of a precious stone, like jasper, clear as crystal. ... The wall was constructed of jasper, while the city was pure gold, clear as glass. The

> foundations of the city wall were decorated with every precious stone; ... The twelve gates were twelve pearls, each of the gates made from a single pearl; and the street of the city was of pure gold, transparent as glass.
> (Rev 21:10-11, 18-21)

... and envisioned Hell as an extrapolation of the worst pains and sufferings experienced on earth magnified many fold ...

> "... It is better for you to enter life crippled than with two hands to go to hell, to the unquenchable fire...where their worm does not die and the fire is not quenched.' For everyone will be salted with fire."
> (Mark 9:43, 48-49)

> The rich man also died ... and from the netherworld, where he was in torment, ... he cried out, 'Father Abraham, have pity on me. Send Lazarus to dip the tip of his finger in water and cool my tongue, for I am suffering torment in these flames.'
> (Luke 16:22-24)

> Thus it will be at the end of the age. The angels will go out and separate the wicked from the righteous and throw them into the fiery furnace, where there will be wailing and grinding of teeth.
> (Matthew 13:49-50)

Jesus provided the above three descriptions of Hell as being a place of fiery torment, but provided no comparable descriptions of Heaven: instead he referred to the "Kingdom of Heaven" and provided similes to illustrate its attributes: like a man who sowed good seed ... like a mustard seed ... yeast ... buried treasure ... a search for pearls ... a net which collects fish of every kind ... the head of a household who brings forth both the new and the old ... a king who forgives the accounts owed him ... a landowner who hired laborers ... a king giving a wedding feast ... virgins going to meet the groom.

In addition to providing no description of Heaven, Jesus taught that the transition from life to afterlife is transformational:

> *Jesus said to them in reply, "You are misled because you do not know the scriptures or the power of God. At the resurrection they neither marry nor are given in marriage but are like the angels in heaven.*
> (Matt 22:29-30)

… and that at resurrection we are no longer in this earthly realm but in an entirely new realm where earthly conceits and concerns no longer exist.

Since Scripture does not provide a single, indisputable description of Heaven or Hell, Christians should not try to impose their preferred versions on others.

On Scriptural Inerrancy

As demonstrated throughout this book, while all Scripture is inspired by God it was written by men with innate human flaws, and this allowed self-serving teachings of Men ("Weeds") to mingle with the teachings of God ("Wheat.") Knowing this, it is up to those who love God to invoke the *Sieve of the Spokesmen* to separate the Weeds from the Wheat.

On Miracles

Just as it is common for religions to demonstrate the divinity of a person with a narrative of the person being divinely conceived, it is also common for religions to demonstrate the power of a god (or god representative) with narratives of their accomplishing miracles. Christians are aware of this in varying degrees, and consequently vary in their assessment of Biblical miracles and their importance: some believe the miracles occurred exactly as written and believing in them should be a litmus test to judge whether or not someone is Christian; some believe Biblical miracles are fables simply written to enhance belief in God/Jesus' power; and others – most Christians – individually pick and choose which miracles they believe.

Nowhere does Scripture teach that believing in miracles is required for salvation, and many places it teaches that caring for our fellowman is all that God requires of us.

What then should Christianity teach about Biblical miracles?

The greatest miracle is that God in His love sent both His Son and the Holy Spirit, the Comforter, to us. To believe in the miracles recorded in Scripture is good, especially those showing

God's power to heal and even raise from the dead, for they provide us with strength, comfort, and hope; to not believe, however, in the light of what we know of human nature, is not a fault, let alone a sin, and our salvation does *not* depend upon it.

On Doctrines, Sacraments, and Rituals

Christianity should recognize and teach that God doesn't desire or require our doctrines, sacraments, and rituals any more than He desired or required Jewish feasts, holocausts, and rituals. Doctrines, sacraments, and rituals serve Man's needs, not God's, and are tolerable only if they're not imposed as a requirement for salvation and don't supplant loving our fellowman. Fighting over doctrines and sacraments has been the primary cause of Christianity's many divisions and subsequent failure to do God's will; quarreling over doctrines must be repented, renounced, and sacrificed in a "bonfire of the vanities."

The doctrines, sacraments, and rituals themselves need not be abandoned – they provide us comfort and bind us together – only our quarreling over them, quarreling over the Scripturally ambiguous, unspecified, or contradictory details.

Consider Baptism for example; the New Testament records:

- a water baptism "for the repentance of sins" by John the Baptist and Jesus' disciples;
- a baptism "in the name of Jesus";
- a baptism "of the Holy Spirit" initiated by the laying on of hands;
- … that those baptized by the Holy Spirit spoke in tongues (as had the Apostles when the Holy Spirit came upon them at Pentecost);
- Mark 16's teaching that …
  "Whoever believes and is baptized will be saved; whoever does not believe will be condemned"
- Matthew 28's teaching that Jesus told his disciples …
  "make disciples of all nations, baptizing them in the name of the Father, and of the Son, and of the holy Spirit …"

The New Testament does not provide a narrative harmonizing these disparate teachings on Baptism with each other and with other New Testament teachings: is the physical act of Baptism required for salvation? … is the physical act of Baptism "magical" in that it requires no knowledge or understanding of the act, as in infant baptism, or does it require understanding and assent, as in adult baptism? … If speaking in tongues is a definitive mark of baptism by the Holy Spirit, why doesn't that occur today except in fundamentalist sects?

Consider also the Lord's Supper:

The New Testament records …

"… the Lord Jesus, on the night he was handed over, took bread, and, after he had given thanks, broke it and said, "This is my body that is for you. Do this in remembrance of me." In the same way also the cup, after supper, saying, "This cup is the new covenant in my blood. Do this, as often as you drink it, in remembrance of me." For as often as you eat this bread and drink the cup, you proclaim the death of the Lord until he comes. Therefore whoever eats the bread or drinks the cup of the Lord unworthily will have to answer for the body and blood of the Lord."
(1 Corinthians 11, repeated in all the Synoptic Gospels)

… but does not state whether Jesus meant "this is my body" and "this is my blood" symbolically, and only wanted future "Last Suppers" to be memorials to his sacrifice, or whether he meant the words literally and was proclaiming that future "Last Suppers" would be reenactments of his sacrifice.

The New Testament does not provide unequivocal answers to these and many other questions, so Christianity over the centuries has made up interpretations of Scripture, sacraments, and doctrines to answer them: the intentions were honorable, but Man's compulsion to fight over its beliefs – its tribal tenets – subsequently caused the splintering of Christianity into its many divisions and invited the derision of the world. … It's now time for Christianity to repent and desist from its destructive warring over Man-made teachings that are unimportant to God.

Imagine, finally, an additional parable of Jesus, a "Parable of the Unfinished Vineyard":

> Now behold, there was a man who cleared land and planted a vineyard. Before leaving on a journey, he told his servants, "I have begun a vineyard which is to grow and cover the entire mountainside. Go, enlist helpers from the surrounding towns and villages; teach them to clear new fields and plant new vines, to care for them even as I have taught you."

> The man departed. When his journey was complete and the time was right, he returned. He found the vineyard had grown but little in his absence and was divided by stone walls into many small fields; the workers in one field would not help the workers in another field, and little was being accomplished. He called his servants to him and asked, "Why has the vineyard not been spread as I instructed you?" And they answered him, "Oh, master, we wanted to, but could not agree among ourselves on what you had meant by some of the things you said when teaching us; so rather than do anything the wrong way, we each did as we thought you wanted."

> And the man said to them ... ?

It is up to you to complete this parable ... and the vineyard.

www.ingramcontent.com/pod-product-compliance
Lightning Source LLC
Chambersburg PA
CBHW070954040426

42443CB00007B/501